ICEBREAKER
MACKINAW
WAGB 83
1944-2006

by Sandra L. Planisek

Great Lakes Lighthouse Keepers Association
206 Lake St.
P. O. Box 219
Mackinaw City, MI 49701
www. gllka.com

ISBN 0-940767-08-2

Cover photo: John Wagner, *Mackinaw* breaking ice in Whitefish Bay, March 2006

Great Lakes Lighthouse Keepers Association
206 Lake St.
P. O. Box 219
Mackinaw City, MI 49701
231-436-5580
www. gllka.com

*This book is dedicated to the crewmembers
of the Mackinaw who made this story possible.*

Table of Contents

Reading the Book

The *Mackinaw* is a fascinating place on several different levels. I was fascinated by everything on the boat from the life style to the engine details, however; I knew that too much depth in any one area might bore the readers. Therefore, I chose to vary the content of the book by mingling chapters on technical details with life stories and lessons offered by the crew.

I let the crewmembers speak for themselves as much as possible. While working on this book I was also video taping crewmembers for later museum displays. So you will notice that they point to something and talk about it. The visual image will be more clear when you come and tour the museum ship.

The reader will have to be alert to the changes in authorship because some times I am speaking and sometimes the crewmember is speaking. I tried to be clear and in cases, where my personal contribution was simply to ask questions, I put those questions in a reddish ink to differ from the actual speaker's black ink. The crewmembers' words are in quotes and are taken verbatim from the tapes. Thus I ask the reader to allow for the informality that is common in everyday language but which you might not expect in a book.

Dick Moehl, President of the Great lakes Lighthouse Keepers Association, and I took most of the photos. Several fantastic photographers donated others and I have written attributions to those authors alongside of the photos. I have been amazed at the willingness of people to share photos that are of the highest quality and costly to create. I really appreciate that. I also need to thank Heinz Wernecke who drew and redrew the wonderful cutaway of the engine for this book and Cidney Roth who read, read, and read the manuscript.

Today's crew is made up of men and women of the Coast Guard. While I tried to always use the phrase "he and she" in the text I am sure I slipped occasionally. I and all the crewmembers know that women are making a huge difference in the Coast Guard and we don't want to intentionally slight them. So please overlook the use of "he" when it should really read "he and she".

I also varied what I called this vessel. Is it a ship, a boat, or probably, more properly, a cutter? I listened to the crew to try to figure what the common usage was and finally I decided that there is no standard. A crewmember might call it a boat in this sentence and a ship in the next. So I did not try to pick one and stick with it. Officially, the Coast Guard calls the *Mackinaw* a cutter.

This introduction must give the greatest credit to the captain, CDR McGuiness, whose philosophy is to allow the public access to Coast Guard operations. He allowed me access to his crew and I took advantage of it. I rode the boat, off and on, from November 2004 until its final icebreaking trip. The crew is fantastic and without their help I would never have been able to write this book. Of course, as the last minutes of putting the book together count down, I am still finding errors. There will be errors and they are mine. It is amazing how difficult it is to listen and get everything right.

I MUST thank the captain and crew. Decommissioning will be a very sad day for me because these 75 new friends will all be leaving. But I will cherish my memories for life. THANK YOU!

Painting the boat "hull red" from stem to stern.

What is the story of the *Mackinaw?*

Cheboygan Mayor Jim Muschell patriotically says that the *Mackinaw* may have tugged the United States back from the brink of defeat in World War II. With his eyes transfixed on scenes only a prisoner of war can know, he admonishes his listeners on the peril our country was facing in 1943 when the *Mackinaw*'s keel was laid. That keel went on to plow open a river so it could flow with iron from the northern mines to the southern steel mills.

Retired crewmembers remember a different *Mackinaw*. They were young, strong, idealistic, romantic, and impressionable when they met her. They were part of something big, something very big, and something important. They gained confidence and pride as they worked on this massive machine. Many of them fell in love and married while in Cheboygan. This was the home where they matured. Twenty, 30, or 40 years later they remember a dreamy time of unbounded happiness and opportunity.

Freighter captains of the past 60 years know the all-powerful *Mackinaw* as a mass of steel, filled with the power and skill to slice and churn ice like no other. When approaching the persistently icy St. Marys River or Straits of Mackinac, freighter captains call Sector Sault for a condition report. Sector Sault will explain the location of the ice and icebreakers. Then the listening captain will always ask, "Tell me again, where is the *Mackinaw*?" She is the ultimate insurance.

Citizens of Cheboygan have seen the *Mackinaw* as a visitor whose personality changes with the captain. Memories abound of the times when this ship harbored virile young men who reached into town and stole the girls away. In recent years the daily news flashes add a dash of excitement to an otherwise quiet town.

Today's crew knows that they have the privilege of working on a war hero. They appreciate both the beautiful ship and the powerful tool. They understand that they have the honor of being the last to tenderly repair and operate this seasoned vessel. Their sense of history is alive.

And, lastly, is the captain who lovingly talks about *Mackinaw*, while everyone else says the *Mackinaw*. He talks of a ship built without compromise to unfailingly achieve the task of national security. He mentions his responsibility

Mackinaw is different things to different people

Chapter 1- What is the story of the *Mackinaw?*

for the safety of this aged and, in some ways, frail vessel. He also understands that *Mackinaw* is a monument: to the war, to the Coast Guard, to the citizens, and to victory. He appreciates that he is capable of preserving that monument past its working years. On his orders, crew members are

leaving their mark on the ship by restoring or decorating some feature. When they return to a museum ship with their grandchildren they can point with pride to their contribution to this vessel.

So what is the story of the *Mackinaw*? It is something different to everyone who touches her. Which story is the most important, which story should be told in a book? My conclusion is that I can only tell my story, what I saw, heard and felt as I had a chance to get to know her. I hope that my story is relevant to you. I was an outsider offered an inside view. Here is what I learned.

Fancywork is part of this crew's legacy.

The Most Unexpected Things

The *Mackinaw* is the pride of the Straits of Mackinac. Residents can recognize this ship at two miles and spout facts on its capabilities for several minutes. I came to the *Mackinaw* with the knowledge that this ship is unique, a

Although the Christmas trees smelled great, the crew continued to find needles until March.

one-of-a-kind icebreaker. I had read about the water-sucking front propeller, the huge ballast tanks that slosh water, and the untarnished record of breaking through all ice. I even had heard that Russians once came to study the design. I knew something about the ship.

I expected my trip to be a detailed look at a very special machine. Instead my trip turned out to be the study of a very special life, living on the *Mackinaw*.

It has been more than a year now since I was living on the *Mackinaw*. Some parts of the experience are starting to fade. But some of the experiences were so unexpected, and some parts so intense, that I will never forget them. These are my memories of sounds, smells, culture, and size of things on the *Mackinaw*.

Smells

The *Rouse Simmons* delivered Christmas trees to Chicago for 25 years before severe winter icing sank the vessel and crew on their 1912 trip. The legend has grown with the discovery of the shipwreck in 1971. In the year 2000 CDR Jon Nickerson decided that recreating the Christmas tree story with the *Mackinaw* would be a good service for the needy, a good exercise for the crew, and an honor to those lost at sea.

I was fortunate to be able to ride along on the 2004 Christmas Tree Ship. The crew had cut 1,200 trees at a tree farm near Cheboygan and had delivered the trees to the ship a few days before our departure.

Early on the morning of November 30th, as we drove between the buoys at the end of Coast Guard Drive marking the entrance to the *Mackinaw's* parking lot, the smell of pine trees surprised me. We were still a hundred yards from the ship where the trees were bundled and covered with a tarp. The smell was fresh and inviting. It was the smell of "up north."

After about two hours I would not notice the evergreen smell again until the trees were unloaded in Chicago. Once the engines were started the diesel smell settled on the outside deck. The *Mackinaw* was built in 1943 - 44 when pollution from 2-cycle engines had not been named, let alone ostracized. The six, 10-cylinder engines pump out a steady plume of smoke and diesel odor.

Once inside the ship the diesel smell is lost in the household smells of food and Lysol. Lunch time and dinner time are easy to identify even if you fail to read the "Plan of the Day." When you smell food, mealtime will follow in 30 minutes. Then dishes must be cleaned. "Sweeping" was the duty of the day for several days on this trip. We were going to be visited by Admiral Papp and possibly Secretary of Homeland Security, Tom Ridge. "Sweeping' brings out the Lysol smell. Cleaning walls, overhead pipes and floors occupied several crewmembers in many corners of the ship. They carried the Lysol smell with them.

We joked that a good souvenir from the ship would a scratch-n-sniff post card with these four *Mackinaw* smells – pine, diesel, food, and Lysol. The only other smell was a whiff of the gray-water holding tanks, but nobody would pay for that.

<u>Sounds</u>

I interviewed the newest member of the crew as he was wandering alone in a hallway. He was carrying a piece of paper with pencil squiggles on it. He said he was following the big red pipe and drawing a layout of the water lines on the ship. Every new crewmember is required to complete a set of drawings in order to learn the ship, meet the crew, and understand the fire suppression system on board. The fear of fire is pervasive. This crew attends fire school in Toledo in the summer and they know how difficult it is to put out a fire. I asked him, "What is the most unexpected thing about this ship?" Just then one of the steady stream of announcements blared from a nearby speaker. "That," he said nodding his head toward the speaker. "The noise. It is everywhere. It never stops. I am having trouble sleeping."

The crew and their family members helped cut Christmas trees on a beautiful northern day

He was right. The noise level was high. Six diesel engines running six generators further running the three motors used to propel the ship create a racket. On top of that there are three additional generators creating electricity for the household uses of the ship. Then there are hundreds of smaller motors running unknowable things. Lay on top of that the alarm bells and whistles that were tested regularly and then the announcements that occurred every few minutes. The noise was deafening. Take that literally. The captain, being concerned for the health of his crew, had ordered a sound-level analysis of the ship. Unfortunately, the analysis has not yet been accomplished and the ship will retire soon. But the crew is prepared with headphones.

The loudest noise was, of course, in the engine room. A foam earplug dispenser adjoining the engine room door is indicative of the sound level. All people in the engine room must wear double ear protection – the foam inserts covered by large headphones.

I am told that when the ship is breaking ice everyone is expected to wear ear protection 24-hours a day. Of course expectation and actuality are not necessarily the same.

While the level of the sound created a tense environment, the information carried by the sounds was of utmost importance. During my initial safety instructions I was told to listen for this alarm and that alarm. Do this if you hear one kind, do that if you hear another. One quick introduction wasn't enough to learn what was what. My first night on the ship I heard an "alarm" every few minutes. I would then listen for the rhythm of running feet that, fortunately, never followed so I would slowly fade back into sleep.

Drawings take a week to complete.

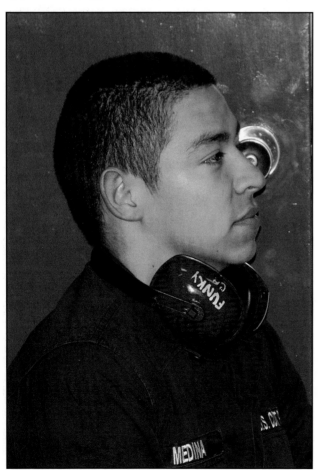

When not in use, ear coverings are worn as a necklace.

Outside each of the three engine rooms is safety equipment including hot pink ear plugs and battered ear muffs.

My initial bunk was toward the midsection of the ship and over one of the engine rooms. The variety of sounds was amazing. There were at least six different engine-type noises starting and stopping at unrelated intervals, plus the alarms and announcements. When I later moved to a forward berth the noise was a drone, the sound of just one engine, and thus much easier to sleep with. This forward berth was call the "wedge" room. This room had a peculiar triangular shape created by the narrowing of the hull on one wall. It made for cozy quarters and I was happy to be on a lower bunk. The steady noise was not a problem.

Our trip took us to Chicago for several days. Then we returned to the Straits of Mackinac to find gale winds blowing. The *Mackinaw* was designed to roll from side to side to help in breaking ice. Ice dampens these rolls. But when there is no ice the rolls are far larger than desirable. The ship will make a stalwart seaman sick in six-foot waves. In a gale the doctor was giving seasick patches to, maybe, 30% of the crew. The captain decided to stop in the lee of Bois Blanc Island and wait out the storm near two anchored freighters and a tug/tow rig. It was evening and the sky was dark so I decided to go to bed. I was fast asleep when I heard "blam, bang, boom, boom, boom", an instant of quiet, and then "boom - boom - boom." Loud and sharp, the sounds were obviously heavy metal beating against more heavy metal. It was right next to my ear. My heart thumped and my mind raced over the possible catastrophes that could be happening. Then the sound stopped, no other unusual noises were to be heard, and finally I realized that we had dropped anchor and the anchor locker was on the other side of the metal wall by my ear. What an experience! The 21-pound chain links are literally ripped out by the falling anchor and beat against the housing as they go. Again, I was relieved that there was no catastrophe.

The mess deck is a place for friendship, education, and for monitoring the sounds of the ship.

Meal time was the time to talk to the crew and learn about the sounds. The mess deck sits over engine room #2. While eating with the enginemen assigned to #2 Space, as they call it, you could see the sounds being processed in their minds. A subtle change in pitch, which I could not discern, would send worried expressions across their faces and the conversation would immediately turn to an analysis of the cause.

The anchor chain runs from its locker below deck to the capstan and out through this housing.

Firefighting clothing is stored just outside the mess deck.

George Keefer

The entire exterior gets scrubbed when the public and the Admiral are coming. Singing still makes the work go easy.

Most troublesome for the crew and me were the messages being broadcast into the high rumble of noise The announcements came at random times and were never repeated. The crew was better prepared to interpret the mumbled messages because they knew the range of possibilities. But it was common for one crewmember to turn to another and ask for the specifics of the message. This

The ship is equipped with several communication devices. Here you see the white telephone and black sound-powered phone.

communication system obviously was a design problem that had never been overcome.

We took on fuel at the last leg of this trip. Fueling is one of the more risky tasks aboard the ship. With fuel being pumped aboard at 630 gallons per minute any small mistake can create a fire hazard and an environmental nightmare. The pumping crewmembers need to be able to communicate with each other even though they are spread from the pumping house onshore to all levels and sides of the ship. MK3 Pietrolungo demonstrated to me the new radio-headphone systems they had tested and would be using for the first time. He was excited that they should be able to hear each other clearly. He also explained that fueling requires two independent communications networks. Keeping different operations on different lines allows the overall manager to be certain that tasks are performed in the correct sequence.

The communication system was the most complex and most important system on the ship. I tried to understand it fully but did not succeed.

While in Chicago the crew scrubbed the total above-deck, exterior of the ship. It was a warm sunny day and everyone was out with long-handled brushes and fire hoses squirting and scrubbing. It was a happy, carefree time and the crew sang a few songs reminiscent of old sailing days. It was a sound of days gone by. That historical image might also have been in their minds because earlier some of them had climbed the mast to tie a Christmas tree to the top. Even though the ship was tied to the dock, they commented on how much the top of the mast swayed. I doubt if you can be in the Coast

The Mackinaw was a beauty docked in Chicago at Navy Pier with Christmas trees decorating her deck and mast.

by the residents themselves. This was like living inside a space capsule.

<u>Mostly I remember the people.</u>

I am embarrassed to confess that I approached the crew of the *Mackinaw* with a prejudice. Who goes into the military? Rambo-types, I thought. I could not have been more wrong. The people I met were NOT uneducated, inarticulate, and macho. They were polite, friendly, very well educated, proud of their ship, and interested in my attempt to understand it.

Why was I so wrong? I tried to find out. I asked everyone I met, "Why are you on the *Mackinaw*?" They explained the Coast Guard system of allowing people to request their assignments based on a list of availability. Ranking in school or personnel evaluations determined who got their first choice. The *Mackinaw* is popular. It draws high quality crewmembers from around the country. Why? It is unique. It has classic Fairbanks Morse engines. It requires classic seamanship. It connects to the day when a sailor was a sailor, not a computer operator. And it carries a happy and devoted crew. What a testament to this war child.

I asked one young seaman, whose name I did not get, why he was on the *Mackinaw* and he went even further in his enthusiasm. "I asked to be on the *Mackinaw* because when

Guard and not be aware of the sailing tales of climbing the mast to raise and lower sails. It was all so appropriate for the Christmas Tree Ship.

<u>Sights</u>

Despite the red hull, most of the ship is painted a rather mundane white or gray. But this does not keep the ship from being a delight to the eye. Every inch of space is covered with mysterious equipment made of brass, steel, leather, and canvas. Real, heavy-duty things that do a real job I assume, since I couldn't fathom the uses of most. Safety gear is brightly colored. Wiring makes interesting geometric patterns. Round brass hatches, leather chairs, and stainless steel bathrooms are all interesting to look at.

Of course, there were also the maritime sights such as lighthouses, buoys, islands, and other ships. I enjoyed these views from the deck but, surprisingly, the crew rarely went outside. Their world was inside the ship unless they had a deck-side duty to perform. Only the navigator was looking at the passing lighthouse and he was only looking in order to get a compass bearing, not to appreciate the historic structure. I thought a Coast Guard career was an outdoor job; it is not. This is life inside a metal world heated, cooled, and lighted

We had a deckside view of the Chicago Harbor Light.

The mess deck is used for studying too.

That leaves eight months each year for the *Mackinaw* to rest, heal, and find recreational activities. People like to look at this massive ship. After the war the *Mackinaw* grew into the role of fashion-model for the Coast Guard. It travels about the Great Lakes doing good will projects and offering tours.

I had not thought about what the crew would do during this off-season portion of the cycle. First, I must explain that the Coast Guard has unique employment policies. All enlisted people serve a 3-year tour and then move on to another station. Officers only serve a 2-year term before moving. The Coast Guard switches people's positions during the summer months to ease the impact of constant moving on family members, especially school children. The result of this policy is that over a third of the crewmembers are new every year. Despite its historic charm, the *Mackinaw* is run with antiquated systems that most new crewmembers have never seen and will never see again in their Coast Guard duty.

Education is the steady beat. Everyone is teaching or learning all of the time. It is more pervasive than any formal school. I had to wonder at the crewmembers who might have thought that enlisting was a way out of the educational system. Instead they entered a world of constant education.

I am old I want to be able to say that I served on the original *Mackinaw*." This historic vessel has built a reputation that young coasties want to rub against.

But in all of the good vibrations on the ship it must be remembered that a crew of 78 young people will always contain a few problems. The ship's "Doc" did not request duty on the *Mackinaw*. She was content in her California position. She was called because the *Mackinaw* needed a senior woman. Now she is providing a stabilizing, motherly influence on the "Queen of the Great Lakes."

When the ship is out of port the crew spends 24 hours a day onboard, living their lives. This total life experience also confounded me. I came to realize that these 78 people constituted a small town which assembled for stints of a few weeks. Every aspect of life occurred onboard. Then, when in port, the crew disbursed to their respective homes and the ship became merely an office building.

The *Mackinaw* is first, last, and always an icebreaker. It does other things, but not always well. Ice in the Great Lakes starts along the shoreline in late December, fills the basins solid by mid-January, and breaks under the spring sun in March only to jam the passageways until April. The *Mackinaw* works at its mission four months of the year.

Work tools like these lines can be beautiful.

Don't get me wrong. I did not see any formal education: no classes, no textbooks. What I saw was one-on-one conversations. The Mechanic Technician 1, MK1, was explaining to the Mechanic Technician 3, MK3, how to clean a valve or repair a gasket. One officer was reviewing the Rules of the Road with another. Everyone's survival on the ship depends on the ship operating properly and it is imperative that the new crew learns his or her jobs quickly. Only steady training assures this.

Education was mixed with evaluation. When someone did not do the job properly they were questioned. If the mistake was technical, the details were reviewed. If the mistake was cultural, they were asked to review their role and commitment. Dialog seemed to be open and information flowed both from the top down and bottom up.

An inexperienced engineering crewman arrived to talk to an engineering officer. He had spotted a fuel leak and was agitated. The officer explained that he had to divert to another fuel line, remove the packing, and replace it. The instruction was informative, direct, calm, and useful. Or a supervisor was questioning a new crewmember. "You were able to get to work on time the first month you were here. Now you have been late several times. What is wrong?"

This was textbook management. Everyone was encouraged, guided, and supported to do their best. I saw no jealousy, no malevolence. I was even more stunned when I read the forms used for evaluations. Everyone is rated on their work competency, leadership abilities, military demeanor, and their professionalism. They know exactly what is expected of them and everyone has the duty to help those around them. Everyone, from top to bottom, must assist those around him or her to get promoted. If your mates don't get promoted, you don't get promoted.

"Deckies" spend the most time outside while handling lines and cleaning.

With a 20-year retirement system and a 3-year rotation there is a steady opening of positions. Everyone has the potential to get promoted in just a few years. What a difference from the business world where job stagnation kills creativity and cooperation. If the majority of the public understood the objective and supportive job environment in the Coast Guard I believe enlistment lines would be long. In fact, later I found out that the lines are indeed long. The Coast Guard is very selective and turns people away.

I would like to introduce you to some of those who were good enough to be selected: the captain who is so quiet, the executive officer who is so disciplined and yet friendly, the young female officers who will rock the Coast Guard as they advance, and at least some of the crewmembers who are devoted to this machine.

Dimensions

So how could I possibly go about explaining the *Mackinaw* in a book that needs to be divided into manageable chapters? The ship certainly can be divided into the above-deck operations and the below-deck work. It can be divided between the work that is science and the work that is art. It can be divided in a rough manner between the neophytes on their first assignment, of which there were many because the *Mackinaw* is a training vessel, and the experienced crew and officers who are skilled enough and numerous enough to handle this labor-driven vessel. It can even be simply

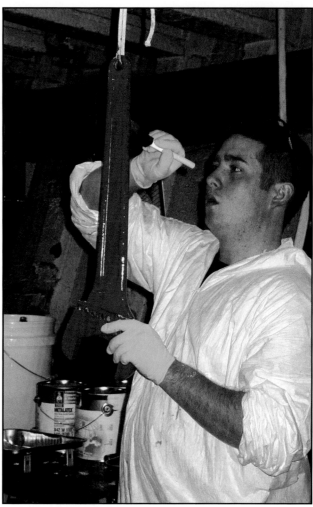

Tools tend to be large on the Mackinaw.

measured, so many miles of this and tons of that. None of these work.

What follows are some of my experiences interspersed with the crewmembers speaking about their lives and jobs. I hope this rather happenstance collection gives you some sense of life aboard the *Mackinaw*.

Just when you think that everything on the boat is huge you encounter a hatch which is very small.

Colorful deck gear.

"Doc"
Claudia Simpson

HSC Simpson sitting on the mess deck.

The first person I met on the *Mackinaw* was the "Doc." I was early for my appointment to meet the captain. The Doc, HSC Claudia Simpson, whose office is perhaps the most central in the boat, was sent to retrieve me from the pouring rain on the quarterdeck. She took me into the wardroom and, acting as the gracious hostess for the boat, offered drinks. She even dragged me around the corner to see the drink dispensers so I could see how easy it would be to get any drink I wanted.

Doc is a smiling, bubbly, blond lady with a caring manner. She acted as the hostess until the captain arrived. When the captain and the XO arrived she left. The captain and XO had a small discussion about Doc being mom on the ship.

She has a steady hand, an ear for listening, and an outdoor voice. She looks after the crew and, like a mom, corrects, and disciplines them as well. Mom with a tough shell.

Later, when I was struggling with seasickness and new-person stress, Doc was the first to open an opportunity for me. She invited me to do an interview while she was giving flu shots. She put me at ease and gave me my first insight into the complex interrelations of the crew.

Doc explained how she and her workers fit into the overall administrative scheme.

"We're the Support Department, the administrative side of the house. The administrative area includes the cooks, the medical support, the paperwork people, and the crew who order all of the supplies. We are all considered the Support Department. Recently we all qualified for the Bosun Mate of the Watch Underway which means all of the support people take turns making sure the ship is secure for sea, that there is nothing lying out, everything is tied down, and the ship is safe for the crew. In the Coast Guard every person has several duties. It is a lot of fun, never a dull moment."

What kinds of aliments does the Doc see?

"We see everything from head to toe injuries. Like last night a crewmember was coming home from a night in Chicago and a shoeshine man attacked him. Now he has a fracture on his left eye socket. They woke me up at around 1 o'clock and it looked pretty serious so I wanted to make sure he wasn't having a cranial bleed. I sent him to the emergency room in Chicago and, sure enough, it wasn't good. Everyone on board said they had never seen an eye like that before. It was pretty serious.

"We've had to make a couple of trips to the emergency room because young healthy guys were complaining of chest pain. A possible heart problem is one thing you always want to take very seriously. We've had a couple of eye injuries. We've had slip and falls and back injuries. Last week, at Christmas tree cutting, the XO cut his finger and we had to do sutures on that. We see a lot of colds and bronchitis this time of year. We see from 2 to 10 people a day, it depends."

"We" included several support crewmen, mostly from the kitchen, which occupies an adjoining space. While I was visiting, the Doc was being assisted by FS3 Johanna Vogel and FS3 Jason Seaburg, both from food services (FS). Johanna was my lower bunkmate and she was invaluable when I first tried to get into my overhead bunk. She gave me detailed instructions on how to pull towards the water main to gain loft while swinging far enough into the bunk to change my grip to a pipe on the back wall for lateral movement. Jason serves as comedy relief in the kitchen and sickbay. He plays the Barney Fife role, thin, frail, and humorous.

Later in the cruise I had opportunities to watch the Doc's medical practice flourish.

The *Mackinaw* is a single purpose boat; it was designed to break ice. I'm not sure of its intended summer use, but riding through big storms was not it. The hull shape produces slow broad rolls even during moderate seas. The passage between Lake Michigan to Lake Huron is foul in almost any wind because your path takes you north, south, and either east or west. Any wind is a problem wind for the *Mackinaw*.

When leaving to go to Chicago we had come headlong into 6-footers as we headed west past White Shoals Lighthouse. As we turned south we had a beam sea that made my stomach call to me. I took a Dramamine, which I got from the Doc, and slept the entire way to Chicago.

After leaving the Chicago Harbor for our trip back through the Straits of Mackinac and on to Rogers City we encountered 15-foot waves in the Straits which produced a 27-degree roll of the hull. The Doc, being privy to the weather forecast, was out suggesting health precautions. It did not take long to realize that I was going to be sick. The Doc came to the rescue. She was dispensing seasickness patches which do not make you drowsy. They take four hours to go into effect

In 2005 and 2006 the crew cut the 1,200 Christmas trees that they delivered to Chicago. The XO, Executive Officer, was very vigorous with his hand saw and cut his finger. Doc was prepared to give treatment.

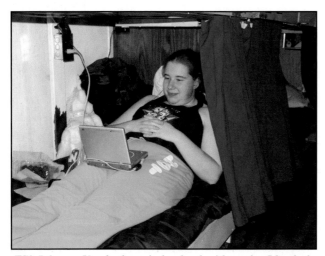

FS3 Johanna Vogel relaxes in her bunk with music. I bunked above her.

and I got mine just in time. They became a fashion statement on the boat with perhaps 25% of those aboard wearing the "bandage' behind their ear. If you have never used one, I would recommend them. Your mouth gets very dry but, apparently so does your inner ear. The patches work.

One of the auxiliarists, who had never been seasick, got very, very ill. The Doc made a "room" call and gave her a shot to get over the sickness. Then she left a patch for later. The crew came through fine, thanks to the Doc's preemptive care.

About the time we began to anchor in the lee of Bois Blanc Island the crewman with the broken eye socket announced that he was considering suicide. Apparently his tussle in Chicago was not a big surprise to his fellow mates as he had had other problems on the boat. As I sat in the dining area, someone rushed forward to the Doc's office. Doc took charge; she came out spewing orders. With a potential suicide, certain military policies were implemented including 24-hour surveillance. The already tired crew were getting extra duties so that a 24-hour companion could be assigned. No matter what he said, he was now a potential suicide victim. He was also a conversation point for the entire crew. He could not be helped "within the framework of a working vessel" so now he was watched 24 hours a day. Someone had to watch him at night, at meals, all of the time. When we got back to home port he was removed from the ship.

Doc talked about some other aspects of her duty.

"The medical service in the Coast Guard consists of doctors and Health Services Technicians. The doctors actually join the Public Health Services and then can be assigned to Prison Services, Indian Affairs, or the Coast Guard. The nearest Coast Guard doctor is in Traverse City. I signed up to be in Health Services and am called a corpsman. It was a long wait to get called for training because there are not many corpsmen in the Coast Guard, maybe 500. The Coast Guard has about 40,000 people in total. As a corpsman you learn how to draw blood, you do IV's, you work in the pharmacy, work in x-ray, you do minor surgery, and you do sick call. There is a lot of training and work in clinics. I was lucky enough to also be trained as a pharmacy technician.

"My greatest challenge is prioritizing the work. I routinely talk to the Executive Officer about the health of the crew. These conversations are confidential. Everyday I have appointments. I also help the crew deal with insurance paperwork.

"I'm also on the damage control training team. We have a cycle. In January we are ice breaking and that is the primary duty. For that I am the Bosun Mate of the Watch Captain. I make sure that everybody's watches are scheduled. If the operations officer has something he would like passed on, I relay that. We also review frostbite and hypothermia training. Come about April, we go into a dockside period to fix the ship. Come May or June we get ready for festivals. That is when we need to start thinking heavily about the CART and TACT – tailored annual cutter training (the name has changed over the years). Navy trainers come aboard to make sure we know how to take care of fire, flooding, electrical problems - any type of damage that could happen on the ship. They always say that the order is to save the ship, the machinery, and then the personnel. But we teach people how to take care of the personnel. We have these green gun bags filled with medical supplies all around the ship, at each engine room, aft part of the ship, forward part of the ship, on the bridge, and the ET shop. My role is to teach people how to be first responders

The walls of the corridors are lined with safety equipment. Here are turquoise frames which can be used to shore up a wall.

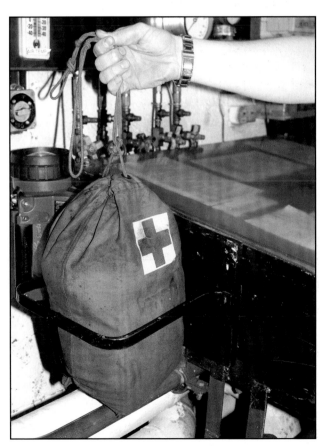

Green gun bags are emergency kits found in every corner of the ship.

This is a typical wall found below deck. It is fitted out for emergencies. At the top are alarm buttons connected to strategic locations onboard. In the center is the grounding wand used to ground electrical current in an emergency. Telephones, whether new or old, are crucial to the operation of the vessel.

The ship's ribbons can be seen just below the conning tower. These are received for each "clean sweep."

and use this. We also have 8 or 10 old Vietnam-era rubber simulated injuries like a sucking chest wound, abdominal wound, burn, and compound fracture. We practice with these simulated injuries. We try to give training throughout the year but we hit it hard in summer. Then comes CART,

The red cap is worn by the Damage Control Training Team. Here one has been left on the counter in the wardroom. Notice the tools of this room; coffee and a telephone.

they check all the paper work. In October we get these Navy riders, and they can be some mean guys. They just look at you and you want to cry. They want to make sure you know all your damage control - how to shore up something if a wall is coming down, how to deflood. We are tested. They come for two weeks. Everybody learns a lot and, if we do good, they call it a 'clean sweep.' We get a ribbon. You may notice the ribbons on the outside of the ship on the conning stations. Every time we go through another training and get a 'clean sweep' we add a gold star on there.

"I like the hands-on part of this job. It is great because I get to do a little bit of everything. I get to see patients. If they have strep throat, I get to do an exam. We have a little test where we can swab the throat. 'Uh-huh, positive.' Put them on antibiotics. I just document everything. I give care under an actual MD out of Traverse City.

"There are a lot of young kids in the Coast Guard and it is hard for them. They are away from their friends and family,

Women at work on the *Mackinaw*

girl friends and boy friends. Sometimes it is just a little bit overwhelming for them, especially around the holiday season. Also they get a little taste of freedom when they turn 21 and start drinking. Some get in trouble with alcohol. We have to send them down to alcohol treatment, a good percent realize the problem, don't do it again and move on. They get a second chance. But a second offender is out.

"They didn't have berthing on this ship for females until 5 or 6 years ago. Now there are about 10 women on board. Some are doing traditional female jobs like cooks and nurses but some are doing the heavy duties like bosun mate and electrician. We have two women officers. It is exciting to see that women can do everything. In the Coast Guard, women can have any job that exists. They are excluded from nothing. That is unlike the other services.

"It is quite common to have a husband and wife in the service. The detailer tries to co-locate them within a 50-mile radius. Don't get me wrong, fraternization is not allowed in the Coast Guard. If I had met my husband on this ship we would not be permitted to date. But once we each had gone to a different station, we could have pursued a relationship. There are times when people fall in love on a ship. It is OK. You just have to tell the Executive Officer and they will separate you. You have to do the right thing. They understand. We have had that situation on the ship before.

"I am proud of the fact that I am the first female corpsman in the 62-year history of this ship and I am the last corpsman on this ship. It is a super crew, a fun boat. The Great Lakes are beautiful. When you are up early in the morning and you see that sunrise over the lake it is just breath taking."

As the Mackinaw prepares to retire the crew is dressing her up. The outdated ribbons are being replaced with the final honors received by the ship and her crew.

Ice Breaking Mission

Designed for the Job

Sitting low in the water the Mackinaw uses her massive weight of 5,252 tons to push open the channels. For icebreaking the ship is loaded with maximum ballast giving it a draft of 19 feet.

Modern icebreaking began in the Straits of Mackinac in 1872. At that time Alpena harbor was iced shut and a call was sent to St. Ignace for help. Commodore Louis Boynton took two ships to perform a rescue. Neither ship could break the ice alone, nor could they break the ice when pulling in tandem. However, when he tied them side-to-side with one going forward and one in reverse, the combination worked. The design of the icebreaker was born: propellers forward and aft.

Over the decades, icebreaking refinements were used in building the ferries that carried railroad cars and automobiles the five miles back and forth across the Straits of Mackinac. Freighters trapped in the twisting turns of the St. Marys River would call the ferries for help. There were so many calls that finally, in 1936, the Coast Guard was charged with

the responsibility of keeping the shipping lanes free of ice. In 1943, World War II demand for steel products sparked construction of the *Mackinaw*.

The *Mackinaw* was designed with all of the best features of the icebreaking ferries. Bow and stern are pointed with a raked angle which allows the boat to ride up onto ice whether going forward or reverse. A reversible bow propeller can suck water from under the ice and lubricate the hull by washing water back along the sides. These were proven technologies in 1943.

But there were new adaptations because the *Mackinaw* needed to be stronger than the ferries. The hull below the water line is of steel plate 1-5/8 inch thick; above the water line it is 1-3/8 inch thick. Although built in the day of Rosie the Riveter there are no rivets in the *Mackinaw*. The ferries had proved that rivets fail under the strain of pounding ice. This hull was assembled with 30 miles of single-bead welding.

The ferries were powered with coal-fired direct drive engines. The *Mackinaw* is powered with diesel-electric power plants. Power from the electric motors can be directed to any of the props so the power can be used where it is needed. The electric motors generate 10,000 hp, but the real measure of an icebreaker is its torque to length ratio. The *Mackinaw* has a ratio of 35:1 vs. the ferries' only 13:1. She has raw power and, with the ability to shift 400 tons of water from side to side in 90 seconds, she has rocking power.

Because she was going to operate like a big tug, she was built with a notch in the stern for towing vessels rigidly against her stern. To help with the towing she is equipped with a towing winch using 2-inch wire cable. The winch has an automatic tension control so that if it feels a surge on the cable, it pays out line. If the pull on the cable drops, the cable is automatically recovered.

The result: the *Mackinaw* works. The *Mackinaw* expands the shipping season by 5 weeks. Year round shipping allows better use of industrial resources such as freighters, steel mills, and employees. Today's just-in-time inventory requires a steady flow of resources. Keeping shipping moving all year keeps America's industry competitive.

This is a picture of the Mackinaw in the spring after ice breaking, which is hard on the paint. To enter the Cheboygan River the ballast water is pumped out and the boat comes in light and high out of the water. You can clearly see the angled Meierform bow. This angled bow line delivers the downward crush that breaks the ice. The bow also has a propeller 12 feet in diameter which either can be used to help with ice breaking or left free wheeling.

USCG photo

The Mackinaw's hull shape is compared to the shape of a football. This broad, round bottom allows the boat to roll left and right to wiggle off the ice. Moving 400 tons of water from side to side will make the boat lean 5 degrees. Because the boat is so wide, 5 degrees seems like a lot. Notice that the bow propeller is sitting off to the side of the boat in this construction photo.

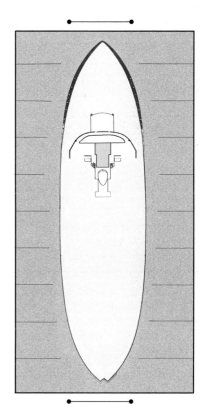

While the bottom of the hull may look like a football, the overall size of the vessel should be compared to a football field. The ship is about the same length and about 1/2 as wide.

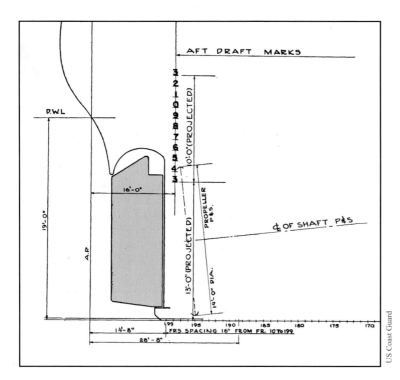

AFT DRAFT MARKS

D.W.L

16'-0"

19'-0"

0'-0"(PROJECTED)

PROPELLER P&S.

13'-0"(PROJECTED)

14'-0" DIA.

A.P.

₵ OF SHAFT P&S

14'-8"

28'-8"

99   195   190   185   180   175   170

FRS SPACING 16" FROM FR. 10 To 199

US Coast Guard

This drawing of the stern of the Mackinaw shows the rudder details.

The Mackinaw has two 14-foot propellers in the stern. The propellers are well protected by pods. In most boats each propeller is followed by a rudder, but the Mackinaw only has one rudder. Since the boat backs up often, a second rudder is a liability because ice could jam between the rudders. Also, the rudder must be protected from the surface ice. An "ice horn" was designed to deflect the ice away from the top of the rudder. Also notice the angled hull line above the ice horn. This brings the ship's weight down on ice when backing.

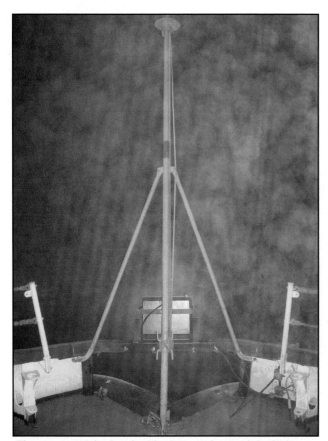

The stern notch is clear in this picture taken at night during icebreaking. A boat is approaching to tie up at the stern.

This photo was taken just after the stern had been repainted. You can see the ice horn and how it curves over the top of the rudder to protect it. The numbers on the hull are depth markers. During icebreaking the hull would be sitting at the 9 mark where the red and black paint meet, indicating 19 feet of draft.

A hull designed for icebreaking is not designed for waves

by MK3 Pietrolungo

"Last year we got caught in a storm on Lake Huron. We were trying to get down to Lake Erie before the storm came and we just didn't make it. We were taking wind and waves on the beam. Because of how wide she is, she heels over real slow. It feels like you are doing more than you are. I was in my rack and my sleeping bag is slick. When we got up on the roll I could feel myself moving a little bit. We were doing 30 degree rolls. The constant back and forth motion will stress metal. Our hot water heater in the scullery broke loose. It sprayed water and put a ground on the 440 electrical system. The steering is tied into the 440 system so we were developing steering problems. The steering short cycled, not getting the degree of movement they needed. Once we secured the power to the hot water system, that took the ground out and the steering was operating normally again. A lot of the cabinets have locking pieces on them so you don't have to worry about drawers coming out at you. Even if we aren't going into a storm, every time we get underway the duty section makes sure everything is locked down. The storm was taking a toll. There was a table in the galley that broke. We had a tall pipe fitting cabinet aft, a heavy cabinet. With the going back and forth it bent the L-bracket that was holding it to the wall and the cabinet toppled over. Luckily, no one was standing there. It took six of us to put it back up. The topper was when a stateroom porthole got blown in. That is when the captain decided 'enough is enough.' We turned around and went back up the St. Marys River. There was still ice in the St. Marys River at the time so we were able to pull into the ice and stay for the night. We went back to the lake the next morning."

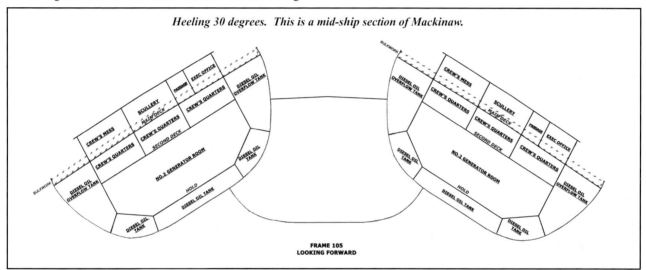
Heeling 30 degrees. This is a mid-ship section of Mackinaw.

When the waves are this high everything gets locked up. Bathroom doors are latched, chairs are roped to desks, bunks are flipped up and anchored and all personal gear is stowed in lockers.

The Schedule

RADM Papp (left) and CDR McGuiness converse during icebreaking. Originally the fleet commodore rode aboard the Mackinaw. Today all icebreaking leaders communicate by cell phone. A visit by the admiral is rare.

By mid-February the ice in the Great Lakes is reaching its maximum thickness. Only those freighters pulled by huge financial rewards dare venture forth. Icebreaking is hard work, both for the crew and the ship. After six weeks of breaking ice the ship needs a check-up so the *Mackinaw* crew plans to spend mid-February to mid-March doing routine maintenance. This is the time to prepare for the truly tough work of spring break-up which usually starts around mid-March.

During this lay-up, called Charlie period, we had a chance to talk to Captain McGuiness.

How is your ship deployed?

"One of the cool things about this job is that when you are eating breakfast you really don't know what you are going to be doing at suppertime.

"Typically, every day the shipping companies or agents for the salt water ships will fax a schedule of where their ships are and where they are trying to go. This fax will go to Sarnia, Canada, which is where Detroit Group (Sector) and the Canadian ice breaking operations are based, and they will fax that same list to Sault Ste. Marie, which takes care of the icebreaking on the north half of the lakes over

to Group (Sector) Milwaukee. The shore folks put the information together and send it to the icebreaker skippers. For example, if we know that we have seven ships upbound in the St. Mary's River and we have no ships downbound, how should we deploy the icebreakers?

"The tactical decision on which icebreaker is going to work where in the river is discussed two or three times a day by the skippers. We probably did it twelve times a day while we were working the *Speer* in 2003. Right now, in 2005, we are doing it primarily by cell phone and conference calls. We discuss what the situation is at each place, what's the best deployment of icebreakers for today, tonight, and tomorrow. The mission is so dynamic that we know that our plans for 48 or 72 hours will never materialize. So it does tend to be a moment-to-moment resource plan."

How does District Nine Headquarters in Cleveland fit into that picture?

"Cleveland is the ultimate resource broker for the American icebreakers. Recently we have been working the northern lakes but in past years we have been down in Lake Erie, the Detroit area, the St. Clair River. If Sault Ste. Marie needs the *Mackinaw* and Detroit needs the *Mackinaw*, who needs the *Mackinaw* more? Cleveland will make that decision.

In March when most of the waters of the Great Lakes are deep blue, the Straits of Mackinac, St. Marys River and Whitefish Bay remain covered with ice. The Mackinaw normally breaks ice in the St. Marys River and then passes through the Soo Locks into Whitefish Bay to open the way for the freighters. After a track is clear the Mackinaw returns through the locks, usually around March 25th, to officially open the locks for the season.

Weather satellite March 26, 2005

"Even beyond that we have an annual cycle to *Mackinaw*. It is ready for ice breaking operations by the first of December with plans to break ice all the way through the end of April. We try to give ourselves a maintenance period in the middle. The boat really needs the Charlie maintenance period because parts break when you are icebreaking. It gives us a chance to shut the ship down and put all of the equipment back together. May, June and July we spend in heavy maintenance. We may take her to a shipyard. We'll bring contractors down and do major maintenance. End of July, August, September, and October are our big training and public affairs months. We show the ship at a number of community events around the Great Lakes. With 50% of the crew being new each summer, we use this time to teach them what their jobs are. Training is perpetual."

Ice Breaking from the Engine Room

Fireman Steve Collins is our guide. Steve is 1-1/2 years out of boot camp, almost two out of high school. He was visibly nervous during the start of our interview. He was "striking" for MK3, a machinery technician. He explained that this means that he is learning from the crew on the boat. Steve is a watch stander in the engine room. The *Mackinaw* has six, 20-piston diesel engines that are cooled with raw water taken from the lake. These engines need massive amounts of fresh air for combustion. This air comes through the engine rooms and passes over the workers before entering the engines. Here is Steve's view of icebreaking.

"I don't really get to see the boat break ice. I don't get to see outside. I'm in the engine room. I stand my watches and pretty much eat or sleep the rest of the day. When we are in ice there is usually a three and one rotation, four hours in the engine room and eight hours out.

Fireman Steve Collins with gauges in the engine room.

Probably the biggest problem in icebreaking is keeping the raw water (cooling water) so it doesn't give you problems. The watch standers in the engine room monitor it. There are special gauges that tell what is going on in different ice conditions.

The raw water you take in through the sea chest cools the "mains" and is discharged back out through the sea chest. That warm discharge water is what keeps the sea chest warm so the incoming water does not freeze up. You have to keep working your valves so you get your mix right.

If the sea chest gets too cold it will ice up. You have to keep cleaning the sea chest strainers until you get rid of the ice. Sometimes these strainers also get seaweed in them. You have to open up the strainers, pull the baskets out and empty them. You just dump it out in the bilge. You build up big mounds of ice in the bilge. Then you adjust your valves to keep the sea chest warmer

We are sucking in outside air. The air temperature outside is the air temperature in the engine room. It gets downright frigid. You're bundled up with as many layers as you possibly can. You are just sucking in snow from outside; it is actually snowing in the engine room. They are pushing in so much air so fast that the engines don't have time to get the air warm. It is just vice versa in the summer. If it is 80 degrees outside, it is pushing in 80-degree air on top of the heat of the engines. It gets fairly warm in the summer."

Can you wear gloves?

"You can wear gloves working with the ice in the sea chest but a lot of the time you are in such a hurry to get it back that you aren't wearing gloves. You hands are turning purple and frozen. Some times your watch isn't exactly fun."

ICE

Saran ice makes no sound.

by Sandy Planisek

The crew on the *Mackinaw* comes from every corner of the country. You hear the full range of U. S. accents onboard. What do these disparate individuals do when they need new words to describe their surroundings? Apparently they lean on the old adage that food is the common language.

Mashed potato ice sounds like ice cubes falling into an empty glass.

Thin plate ice looks and tinkles like glass breaking.

Mackinaw tradition has built a food-based vocabulary to describe the types of ice found by icebreakers. You have Saran ice, mashed potato ice, pancake ice, snow cone ice, and margarita ice. Each of these types of ice also creates a unique sound and applies a unique vibration to the hull. If there were words for these I never heard them, but I have added my own interpretations of the sounds of ice on the *Mackinaw.*

When the Mackinaw hits solid sheets of ice that extend for miles in all directions the ice groans and squeaks under the pressure she applies. Imagine the squeak from chewing on ice cubes.

You can just make out a ridge in the ice where the track disappears. These ridges can be 15 or 20 feet thick and are created by winds stacking the ice up. The ridges can slow and stop the Mackinaw but she merely backs up and rams again, getting through. Cutting through a ridge sounds like rocks tumbling inside a clothes dryer.

All of the substantial ice patterns cause the hull to vibrate. OSHA requires that all crew working in the forward half of the ship wear ear protection during icebreaking. The vibration destroys light bulbs so a huge supply is put aboard for ice season.

The Mackinaw is turning the rows of pancake ice (the round pieces with turned up edges) into snow-cones.

John Wagner

Operation Taconite

Press Release: March 2006 Sault Ste. Marie - *Spring breakout on several area shipping channels will begin in earnest on Friday, March 17, and continue through March 22, according to announcements issued by the Coast Guard on Tuesday. The ice work by a number of U.S. and Canadian icebreakers will open ice-covered channels from the Straits of Mackinac up the St. Marys River and across Whitefish Bay a few days in advance of the season opening of the Soo Locks on March 25.*

On Friday USCGC Mackinaw and CCGS Samuel Risley will pass upbound through the Poe Lock to open channels above the Locks. While Mackinaw breaks out the steamer channels west and northwest of the Locks, Risley will continue across Lake Superior to break out Thunder Bay, Ont.

As she has throughout her long career, Old Mackinaw will set and groom steamer tracks through the upper St. Marys River and out across Whitefish Bay. Old Mackinaw, now 62 years old, will be making her last icebreaking sortie into the familiar upper river and Whitefish Bay ice.

- by Sandy Planisek

On March 17, 2006 it was very sunny but the car registered only 4 degrees on the drive up to Sault Ste. Marie to meet the *Mackinaw*. I had a chance to ride the old *Mackinaw* as it passed through the Poe Locks. The Canadian ice breaker *Samuel Risley* went through with us.

We entered the locks at 9am and there was hardly any ice in the lock itself. We tied up to the lock wall but the *Risley* did not. We rode together to the edge of the ice field near Ile Parisienne. These two big red boats made a beautiful site against the white snow and blue sky.

It was a bumpy, noisy ride, typical of icebreaking. When we hit the windrows we stopped and put all six engines online. We traveled about 60 miles, round trip. It took us 7 hours and we burned 2,305 gallons of diesel, meaning we burned about 39 gallons per mile traveling on average 8-1/2 miles per hour.

It was obvious that everyone thought this was a special trip. There were 50 guests aboard and lots of video crews including PBS. Crew members who worked in the engine room took this opportunity to come out and look over the bow at the icebreaking. There were smiles all around.

The Mackinaw has broken the track through the Poe Lock and the Risley is not far behind. This annual spring breakout is called Operation Taconite because it opens the path for iron ore carriers leaving the docks in western Lake Superior headed for the steel mills of the lower lakes. Taconite is the name given to the partially processed iron ore pellets these boats carry.

Edgar B. Speer and the Rock Cut 2003

Notice the people standing on the shore watching

by CDR Joe McGuiness

"That was the first time the crew that came on with me was running all six engines together, all three shafts together. We were running all our different combinations of power and thrust to get the 1,000 footer through what had to be 10 or 12 feet of mashed potatoes. That is what that ice was like by the time we were done milling it. You can see where we have broken the surface ice and all of this has been milled by us before. It was like a snow cone from the local Seven-Eleven or like mashed potatoes, thick and sticky.

CDR Joe McGuiness has the honor of being the last skipper of the Mackinaw

"Usually what happens is the freighter is plowing a big plug of ice in front of the ship. When they approach the Rock Cut, which is shallower and narrower, it is like entering a funnel. There is no place for the ice to go, so some of it rolls deep beneath the ship. The freighter drives itself up on the ice and gets stuck. The *Speer* was actually aground on ice.

"We tried two extraction methods with the towing cable. Freighters are required by the International Maritime Organization to have a pre-rigged emergency towing pendant so if they lose power they can be towed. We slid underneath his bow to where his pendant hangs and attached our towing cable onto their pendant. We kept slow power astern to keep us tight against the ship until we had a solid connection."

How do you get that close?

"Well the good thing about icebreaking is that ice is all solid. It is consistent. It is goopy. You can just power your way right back in under the bow. When you take the power off, the icebreaker stops in place. We don't have drift or momentum issues. We were probably using close to 6,000-horse power just to move us. So if you are using 6,000 horse power just to move at one or two miles per hour, when you take the power off you just stop pretty much instantaneously.

"We broke four or five of the freighter's emergency towing pendants trying to get that ship out. *Mackinaw's* cable is 2 inches in diameter and freighters use 1-3/4ths, so the freighters always break first."

Can they drop another one down?, I asked.

"Yes, but it's not as easy as it sounds. It takes two hours of pretty substantial work to get it rigged in place.

"At some point we tried to tow the ship out. We actually got the *Speer* moving on one of the tow attempts...but...when it did finally move, so did all the ice in the Rock Cut which had re-frozen to her sides. Shortly after that the tow parted.

" Later we tried to hold the icebreaker in place and blow our prop wash down the freighter's bow and along both sides. We hoped that this would drive the ice out or melt the ice away. The bottom of the river, the earth, is about 50 degrees so the water at the bottom is warmer. The surface water is close to freezing and the air, when we were doing this, was minus 25F at night and minus 19F during the day. Our ice breaking efforts had about a 45 minute life span. Then the open water all froze back up and we had to start over.

"At some point we decided that this operation had turned into a salvage mission because the ship was essentially aground and we were not going to get it out. We had broken up all of the surrounding ice. The *Mackinaw* is a 10,000 horsepower ship. They brought in two 15,000 hp commercial tugs and a 5,000 hp commercial tug. The ship itself has 19,000 hp. So roughly 55,000 hp was used to extract the *Speer*. The tugs took it out in three shots. They moved it about half a ship's length, then they moved it about half a ship's length again, and then they finally got it floating. In the meantime, we had shifted our mission from trying to actually pull the ship out to grooming the ice so when they finally did get moving they had some place to go."

The propellers can make a froth, turning the navy blue water turquoise.

Milled ice along the edge of the solid ice pack.

USCG photo

You can just see the cable between the vessels. They are shackled together close to the Speer. At this point the Mackinaw is at full throttle to create prop wash. The cable is merely holding the Mackinaw in place near the Speer. This process caused the bow of the Mackinaw to rise up. The crew still comments on the difficulty of trying to walk forward on the rising decks.

Ode to the Lady of the Lakes

by LTJG Molly Killen in tribute to the Mackinaw's effort to free the Speer

Water churns, and fuel burns as 10,000 horses roar.
The maelstrom aft from turning shafts renders the brash no more.
70,000 pounds are tightly wound about the drum of her towing winch,
and her howser wire, while under fire, displays not the slightest flinch.

A six-foot tide at the prow resides, while beneath the beset vessel's keel,
The icy morass succumbs en masse to the power of blades of steel.
The violent attack upon the pack of the icy, iron vice astounds the observer,
master and learner, as we tensely await the price.

BOOM goes the pendant, but our lady, resplendent, and all of her gear are whole.
Our heart rates rise as we surmise about her awesome power's toll.
The bards who told of heart of gold only sailed upon wooden keels,
And never measured the priceless treasure that is our Lady's heart of steel.

We have but to ask if we are to bask in the aura of her warrior spirit.
'Tis merely air that brings to bear that which we ask, even as we fear it.
BOOM sounds twice, BOOM tolls thrice, as two more pendants die.
This warrior queen, as we have now seen, will defeat her woven, steel ties.

My account isn't done, as this is but one of the Lady's countless feats.
She's astounded her crews, grizzled and new, for the past six decades, at least.
In my short time on this ship of the line, I've watched her destroy and dance.
The likes of this queen are seldom seen unless genius and need meet by chance.

Molly said it was a good watch if, when it was over, her hands were green from the brass throttles.

Strategy

by CDR McGuiness, January 2005

"We were waiting at Green Bay last year and used that time to let people practice ship handling. There is a magic line in the sand, business-wise, where the Federal government will break ice, and private business will break ice. At Green Bay it is right off of Sherwood Point. We did what you might call a 3-point turn at this point. It was good practice because we use the same maneuver in the St. Marys River. It is not a fancy maneuver but it is difficult to do in the ice because the ice provides so much resistance to the twisting hull. Once we had the tracks laid down it gets easier because the boat wants to stay in the tracks. The difficult thing about teaching ship handling in icebreaking is that sometimes the ice is moving the ship more than you are, giving you all kinds of grief. It is a frustrating environment to teach in. This was a good chance to let the crew practice.

"Ideally, you have time to establish tracks. I prefer to get to the river a day before the freighter comes. Trying to turn the ship in the ice wears on you. There is a lot at stake there. If you do that the day before and get the track boundaries marked, escorting a freighter the second day is a lot easier. If you arrive and ships are waiting, then you have to move ships. I'd rather plow the road before the traffic comes out instead of plowing right in front of the school bus.

"The *Mackinaw* does the heavy stuff, pushing things out of the way. But the smaller icebreakers, the 140s, are really maneuverable. They can spend a whole day circling in one turn chopping the ice up. We might only be able to make two or three passes in a day. Typically, the season starts with the *Mackinaw* in Whitefish Bay because the ice is heavy there. Last year we started with five days in the lower river to help prepare tracks. Then we went up to Whitefish Bay by ourselves. We are doing the same thing this year. We spent two days running tracks in the lower river assisting with the heavy work down there. Now we will move to Whitefish Bay. Whitefish Bay is generally a straight run, unlike the river, but the enemy up there is wind. If you get a big west or big east wind it creates pressure that closes the tracks a little and then the ice rubs on the freighter's hull and creates friction that the freighter does not have the power to overcome.

"If you have to break out a ship, you come up and swing around it. If you stay too far from it you don't have an effect on the ice holding their hull. If you come too close you risk a collision. There is a lot of art in it. You get to know the different characteristics of ships and you get to know the different characteristics of the masters. Two masters of the same ship will operate it very differently. Some are going to get through the ice no matter what. They might think, 'Would you please get that icebreaker out of my way?' Other masters are a lot more cautious. There are folks who are cautious to a fault, and there are folks who have bravado to a fault.

One of the 140s has spent the day working with the Mackinaw. They have decided to hove-to together for the night. This means they have pulled into the ice field perpendicular to the track and will allow themselves to be frozen in for a safe overnight anchorage. The Mackinaw will easily be able to break both ships out in the morning.

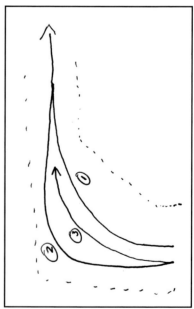

This is the captain's drawing of breaking ice in a restricted curve. The dashes are shallow water. The Mackinaw first proceeds on the inside of the curve, then backs along the outside of the curve, then proceeds down the middle.

"If we are breaking ice in a sharp curve in the St. Marys we first cut the inside of the curve. Then we work astern along the outside edge of the curve. We judge how much acreage we have to break depending on the freighter. Obviously for a 1,000-footer you have to break up a lot more, maybe five passes back and forth. For a small tanker, often one pass is sufficient if we turn slow enough.

"When a 1,000-footer turns this curve it pushes ice up against the outer edge. If the ice is hard enough the 1,000-footer will try to keep his bow on the inner curve. Our daily maintenance is working the outside of the curve. The good thing is the outside of the curve is where the good water flow is. So even though the freighter is packing the ice up, nature is eroding it at the same time. You learn pretty early in the maritime trade that you are a fool to work against Mother Nature."

by LT Wyatt

"The first thing you learn about driving a boat is only go as fast as you want to hit something, especially when you are maneuvering around a pier. An icebreaker is completely different. When you are breaking ice, hit it as hard as you can and break it. And if you don't break it, back up and hit it again. That is what is fun about breaking ice. It is like sitting inside a 55-gallon drum while someone beats on it with a hammer. It is noisy and not exactly comfortable. It will vibrate a lot. It takes some getting used to but it is fun."

by LCDR Barner in a email, March 2006

"We hove-to last night but the plate drifted two miles. I'm not sure about tonight. We may drop anchor tonight.

The last phase of ice decay is occurring - chaos."

The Mackinaw making wide, smooth curved tracks for the freighters to follow.

The Michipicoten was stuck and the Mackinaw is circling to open some water before backing up in front of the freighter to provide a leading escort.

Big Bertha

The cable is fed across this pulley.

Wrap 1,800 feet of 2-inch plough steel woven cable on a 5-foot drum, anchor it to the floor with massive springs, add modern controls which allow you to roll out and retrieve the cable automatically with a powerful DC motor, and you have Big Bertha, *Mackinaw's* towing machine. Modern controls allow the operator to set a constant tension on the cable or to set a constant length of cable played out. The machine adjusts for the tugging a towed vessel creates.

During a practice towing maneuver the cable was run to a Coast Guard 140-foot icebreaker. These small 3,500 ton icebreakers are considerably lighter than the 60,000 ton taconite carriers. When the towing cable was attached to the small icebreaker, the *Mackinaw* pulled forward to put a safe towing distance between the vessels. The weight of the towing cable was so large compared to the weight of the vessel in tow that as the *Mackinaw's* crew played out the cable, the cable sank deeper and deeper into the water and its weight pulled the tow closer and closer. It was clear that this towing cable is only to be used on the really big ships.

The cable comes out of the winch room and runs across the pulley in the center of this unit then goes aft to the stern of the ship. At 7.4 pounds per foot the cable from the winch to the stern weighs about 1,000 pounds and takes all of the deck crew to support it.

The cable is laid up tightly on the drum by the spooling mechanism on the left side of this photo. Notice the man's hand at right for a size comparison.

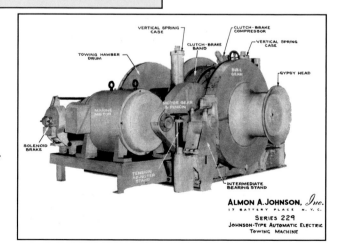

This winch is really three winches. The gypsy head can operate independently of the big drum and pull synthetic line for small jobs. The big drum is wound tight with 2-inch plough steel cable. This cable is used for towing big items like freighters and, as explained earlier, for holding the Mackinaw in place when her engines are operating at full power.

Towing

by MKMC Hamerle

"I was onboard when we tried to pull the *Edgar B. Speer* out of Rock Cut. That was a real interesting experience. We pulled and we pulled. I saw the towing winch flexing in its mounts, considerably. It has 80,000 pounds of line pull and it was rolling up and pulling off the deck. If it wasn't that we were using the *Speer's* pendants we could have done some real damage to our ship. Three times we parted their smaller pendant. The pendant is the length of cable that goes between their bow padeye, welded to the front of the ship, and our towing cable. They would shackle their cable to their padeye and we would shackle that to our cable. We worked on it for two days. I've seen pictures that were taken where our bow is up in the air and there is a lot of propeller wash. The *Speer* was stuck hard and they had to get ice-capable tugboats in there to break all the ice. They also flushed two feet of water down the locks to raise her up."

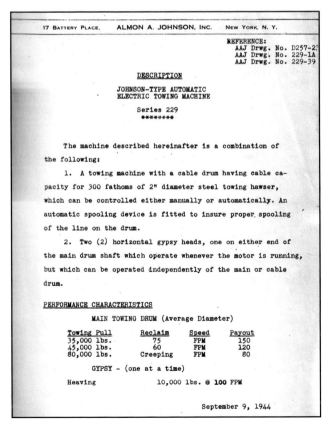

The pulleys are run by a planetary gear system. The winch can pull 80,000 pounds, the steel cable is rated for 120,000 pounds.

The Whitefish Bay Crab Walk

Bank-cushion, a narrow-channel shallow-water phenomenon, also occurs during icebreaking. It becomes a navigational problem when trying to free a freighter stuck in the ice.

The *Mackinaw* circles the stuck freighter and then pulls ahead of the bow. It then backs right up to the bow of the freighter and pours on the power to create a huge wash of water past the sides of the frighter. This usually pushes away the ice holding the freighter.

The crab walk occurs when the *Mackinaw* is backing up to the freighter. Backing up until you touch a freighter is a dangerous maneuver. In this process the stern wants to bounce away from the solid ice and back into the track it has just made. Bounce-cushion causes it to back up in a crab walk fashion.

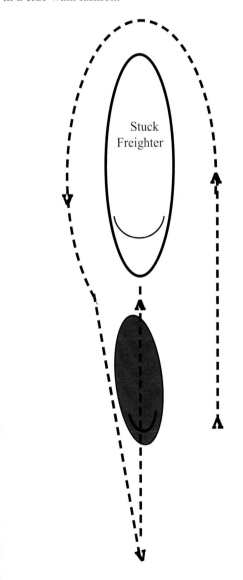

The Samuel Risley, a Canadian icebreaker, passing Gros Cap Reefs lighthouse on its way to Thunder Bay.   The icebreaking partnership with Canada was celebrated with the Mackinaw's last public appearance in Sarnia, Canada.

First Lieutenant Nikki Wood

by Nikki Wood

What are the duties of this office?

"I am the First Lieutenant onboard which means I am the division head for the Deck Division in the Operations Department. As the First Lieutenant I directly supervise a Chief, a Bosun Mate First Class, and underneath them about 15 non-rates. Deck Division takes care of painting on the ship, the upkeep of all deck equipment, all of the mooring lines, basically the stuff that is topside. My deck guys have something to do with anything that isn't engineering. They merged one of the navigation rates, quartermaster, with one of the deck rates, bosun mate. Now they are both considered bosun mate and are getting to cross qualify on the bridge as a BMOW, Bosun Mate on Watch. The majority of the crew for the small boats comes from the deck division. My guys make up the coxains, the boat crew, and the people who handle the 'falls.' Some engineers come onboard too. The deck crew does small boat checks every day and performs upkeep on the small boats. They have a lot of responsibilities. They have a lot to do.

When they first come on board the Chief decides where he wants them to go. People who have priority are the people who have the highest ranking and have been onboard the longest. They get dibs at the primo positions like rescue swimmer. A lot of people want to be the rescue swimmer.

George keefer

LTJG Nikki Wood shown here doing the dreaded paperwork.

They have to pass qualifications. Another desirable job is master helmsman for tough evolutions."

What is a tough evolution?

"Anything like mooring up, getting underway, general emergency drill. It is important to have your best people in

Small boats are part of her responsibilities.

the positions that are important or necessary. Mooring up and getting underway we do all the time, but it is a tough evolution. There is a risk as opposed to driving down the middle of the lake where all you are doing is driving a straight line. If we are off by five degrees in the big lake it is not going to make a big difference. If we are in the channel and we only have 300 feet to play with, being off by 5 degrees is going to make a huge difference."

In your job what are the biggest problems?

"After college, before I came to the Coast Guard, I worked in a civilian job. I had about a year and a half experience in a professional job. One of the biggest problems in any workplace is communication. I think this crosses all employment boundaries. Making sure the people who you supervise know what is going on. And making sure the people you work for know what is going on. Poor daily communication with people can lead to personnel problems or can lead to uncomfortable work situations. It is all just a matter of miscommunication or poor communication. I think that is one of the biggest difficulties in any job. I may have a bad day because I forgot to do something, but that is rare or passing. The big repetitive problems come back to communication."

Opportunities?

"The best part of my job is anything that doesn't require me being in my office doing the paperwork, away from the marks, all the stuff that is behind the scenes. I like to be on the bridge. I like to be driving the ship. I like to be breaking out other vessels. That is what I like to do. That is the top position on this ship. It is the most fun. You have the most contact with the captain. In my opinion that is the best job on this ship. And because I am able to work that job and I feel that I am somewhat competent at it at this point, it is very fulfilling and challenging at the same time. There are days when it is disappointing because I thought I was further

Here the deck crew pulls in the electric cord before leaving the Cheboygan dock.

along than I was. Being on the bridge and being able to make a decision on short notice and not bursting into tears is something I developed here. That confidence opens up opportunities for me beyond the Coast Gaurd. When I first came onboard I was very nervous about being on a ship and not knowing what to do. Having someone coach me on how to drive would make me very nervous. It has been a year and a half of doing the moorings and being underway, and having my own watch and dealing with all the problems that happened on my watch, and disappointing the captain and doing some things wrong. Now I have grown to the point that if I do something wrong I get a little pissed off but then I realize that I can correct it. Then, hopefully, it won't happen again. It has given me twice as much confidence as I had and that is a lot. Just putting up with all of the military stuff gives you more confidence on the bridge, gives you more confidence in your personal life. It builds and develops you as a person. Those have been the major opportunities."

Why did you choose the Coast Guard?

"I spent three to six months sitting in my civilian office staring out of my window when I ran out of work to do and thinking, if I stay here my life is going to turn into a life of monotony, which is what I was completely afraid of. My Dad was in the Navy. He always said that the Coast Guard looked like a really good deal to him. Every time I tell Navy people that they laugh. Because he said good things about the Coast Guard, I looked into it. He always told me go OCS, make sure you go as an officer. So I looked into Officer Candidate School. I applied to them. There were some medical complications. I have Duane's Syndrome in my eye so my application process was extended to about eight and a half months. It was 8-1/2 months of sitting around wondering where is my life going. Am I going to get into the Coast Guard, yada, yada? That was the reason I joined up. I didn't want to have a boring life. I wanted to have some part of my life where I did something somewhat exciting. "

Has it worked out?

"Yeah, it has. I am driving a 290-foot, 5,000-ton ship. That's pretty exciting when you are not dealing with the monotony of this job."

Once you got through school how did you end up on the *Mackinaw*?

"I was at OCS 17 weeks. Probably halfway through they give everybody a list of all the available billets for that class. I knew I wanted to go 'underway' because I wanted to do something exciting. Underway sounded like the most exciting thing. They only have certain ships that take females. I had originally put in for the *Polar Star*. I didn't get that but I got the *Mackinaw*. "

What is the most unexpected thing?

"The most unexpected thing is that I learned that I really love my hometown. I had wanted to get out of there and get away. Being away from there made me realize that I really love my friends and family. I miss them a lot. I didn't figure that would happen. Everybody else grows up and moves away but I have learned how much of a priority friends and family are in my life. I have learned that the fun and action and chaos of a crazy life with a lot of challenge in it is less important to me than being around my family and friends."

What is your most memorable experience on the *Mackinaw*?

"I'm sure there have been a ton but what first comes to mind is last year in the icebreaking season Molly Killen, another LTJG onboard, and I sat on the fantail after one of our watches. We developed a routine of doing that. In ice-breaking season you stand your watch and then you relax because it is so draining to break out ships and work in the ice. We would get our portable chairs out there and bundle up and just sit and talk. You can hear the ice crashing around you in this nice, serene atmosphere. How proud we are that we really like the hardship of it - being tired, being exhausted from the breaking out - but still being glad that we were there

and enjoying the whole experience. Just sitting back there talking with her about how glad we were that we were on the *Mackinaw* is a good memory."

Do you have any special stories?

"I hated OCS when I was there because it was an indoctrination program. It was supposed to be tough and it was supposed to push you. It was supposed to weed out the bad seeds. I hated it, I didn't like it, and I didn't think it was effective on me. At the end I said, 'Well there was probably no other way they could do it.' I'm feeling the same way about here. You get into the daily routine where you come in at 6:45 in the morning and you've got six inches of paper sitting on your desk and there are some projects you are avoiding because they are aggravating to do and you don't want to put the time into them. That starts to become the focus of my job, all this paperwork. At the end of my tour I am going to realize that I miss walking through this passageway. I miss fighting over the head with Molly. I miss trying to duck out of the wardroom to avoid all the VIP luncheons. I'll miss all these small things and I am not taking the time to burn them into my brain as a memory right now."

What is next for you?

"This spring I am supposed to transfer out and go to another billet. Because I came through OCS I only have three years of obligation in the Coast Guard. What I will probably do

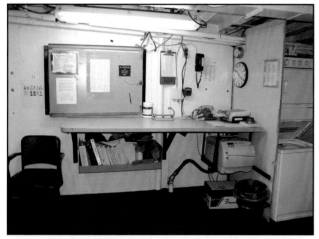

The corridor through officer country passes through a shipboard office with a fax machine, damage control boards, and washer/dryer.

either at my three-year mark or shortly thereafter, in four or five years, is get out of the Coast Guard. I am thinking about opening my own business. I know that I need to work for myself.

I always thought I would go back home but other things start to affect you and pull you. You build relationships with other people and that becomes important as well as your relationships with your parents and friends.

Is there anything else you might want to tell to people, especially girls?

"The *Mackinaw* has been exceptionally good to females, almost to the sense that there was no gender aboard. At least I felt that way in the wardroom. Molly and I have integrated as best you possibly could. I think it is a unique situation for a female to be in where she can let it all hang out. You can basically do that here because there is no gender gap. There is no expectation that you are going to show up for watch with earrings, makeup on, and your hair done right. There is an expectation that you show up for watch and do your job."

By the time this book went to press Nikki was out of the Coast Guard.

Life Onboard

by Sandy Planisek

I am an experienced world traveler and have lived in very primitive conditions in Southeast Asia, so why was my heart pounding so hard as I stood on the deck of the *Mackinaw* watching the Cheboygan parking lot recede? I was only going to be onboard for 10 days for the Christmas Tree Ship trip to Chicago. How hard could this be?

It certainly felt like being in a foreign country: the language was foreign; the dress was foreign; the activities were foreign; even the demographics, young and predominately male, were foreign. But that did not seem like enough to explain the profound, empty feeling I was experiencing. In retrospect I think it was because I was undertaking this adventure alone, no husband, no friend.

This makes me empathize with the 100s of new recruits who have stood at the bottom of the ramp looking up at his or her future home. Even I was asking, "Will I fit in?'

The first step from the dock to the ramp is a step into and onto a new world. Starting with the new language, the

A security watch stander inside the quarterdeck office. While in ports where the public will be visiting the crew often wears their "Bravos," the dress uniform seen here.

The brow is the ramp up to the main deck of the Mackinaw. The quarterdeck is the area at the top of the brow. The little room with a window and door is manned 24 hours a day by the security watch stander. Protocol says that a visitor stands to the right side of the brow and asks permission to come aboard. The ship-board host comes and escorts the visitor onto the ship.

ramp is called the brow, etymology unknown. It is unlike any walking surface I had seen before with mini-I-beams bolted across at about foot intervals. I presume this is to give good traction in snow, but the strange spacing of these boot scrapers assures Fred Astaire won't gracefully sweep up this gangplank.

Once onboard, a stroll around deck is nice. It is decorated with numerous puzzling machines all of which, I am sure, have duties assigned to them. The deck is also filled with trip hazards: tie down places, cables stretched from here to there, bases of machines. A vigilant eye is necessary.

The brow presents a walking challenge.

The bow deck is covered with air intakes, winches, cables, hatches, spray shields, masts, and scuttles.

The aft deck is particularly tricky to walk. Notice all of the little things sticking up from the deck. As you are watching them you can easily walk into the head-height towing bar. This bar is removed in summer for safer walking.

After you have puzzled on deck for an hour or so you may want to actually enter the vessel. There are no door handles, probably because there are no doors. A large lever often opens the watertight hatch, which is really not a door at all. High sills are present on every hatch. How many combinations of six door levers and four sill heights can an engineer design?

Not all hatches are door-like. Some are in the deck and open to a ladder through which you descend directly to the next lower level.

I estimate that there are 30 hatches going from the outside to the insides of the *Mackinaw*. The boat is a bewildering array of narrow passages with latched doors to hidden spaces. There seems to be a protocol at each door. Some require knocking; some require hats on or hats off. Only subtle differences tell you just where you are. It took several days to be able to find my sleeping quarters. The 7-story boat certainly has more rooms than people. So in wandering about it is easy to find yourself in a space with no one around to provide directions.

After about three days I realized that the designers had even planned for disorientation. On nearly every wall space, called bulkheads, is a reflective sign with a string of numbers. Once trained, you can break the code and decipher your location within the hull. The numbering scheme, coupled with the fact that the most important places on the boat - the mess deck, doctor's office, and log office - are located in the center of the boat on the main deck, offers some hope of orientation.

It can be disconcerting to see a head pop up out of one the deck hatches.

The passages are narrow and cluttered with safety gear.

LOCATION CODES

deck number - frame number - position relative to centerline - compartment use

Deck number = the main deck is number 1, the next deck down is 2, etc. Above the main deck are levels and they are numbered with a 0 in front. So the level above the main deck is 01

Frame number is the number of the rib of the boat starting at the bow and moving backward. The ribs are 16 inches apart. The frame numbers run from 0 to 210.

Position relative to centerline zero for things on centerline, odd for starboard, and even for port.

A lever door opener and a wheel door opener are typical.

The wheelhouse is on the 3rd level above the main deck and forward, on the 76th frame, on the boat. This particular door is on the port side.

A guest said to me, "I really feel like I am learning my way around. I think I have figured out how to open the door."

Map of the main deck of the *Mackinaw*

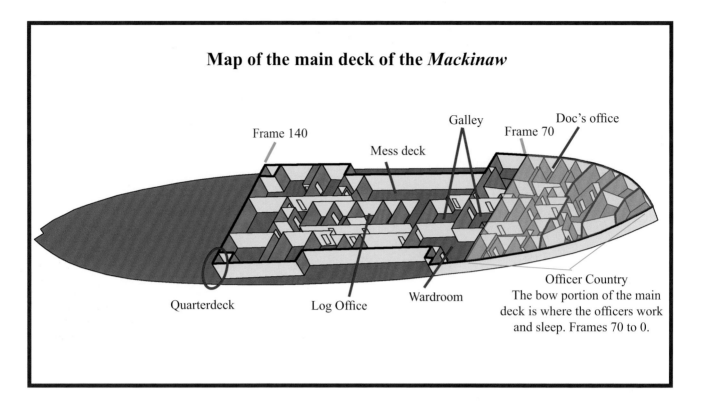

Frame 140

Mess deck

Galley

Frame 70

Doc's office

Quarterdeck

Log Office

Wardroom

Officer Country
The bow portion of the main
deck is where the officers work
and sleep. Frames 70 to 0.

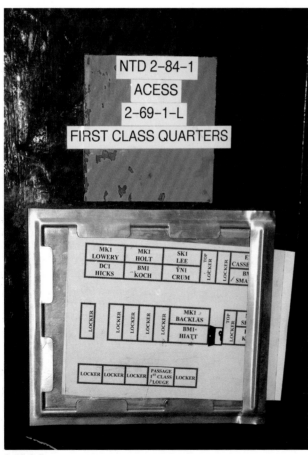

2-69-1-L
This room is one deck below the main deck, towards the front, on the starboard side of the boat and it is living space.

2-141-3-Q
This room is also one deck below the main deck but towards the back and it is starboard also. Q is for miscellaneous use. Even the light switches, at left, are hard to identify. This is the ship's store. Crew can buy clothing, toiletries, and candy. This captain forbids the store to sell cigarettes.

Stairs and Ladders

Looking down. Staircases vary from steep to vertical. Hand holds vary from pipes, for quickly sliding down, to chains which are worn smooth from use and offer a palm massage as you slide down.

Looking down. This type of staircase is the most challenging. Notice the handholds to the right, above the wheel and to the left, below the wheel. You step over this hole onto the ladder while holding those two handholds.

Looking down. This type of ladder is common below deck. It is not a problem for the young crew.

Looking up. This stairway, with chain handrails, is being prepared for new paint.

Berthing

by Sandy Planisek

You don't realize the number of closed doors on the ship until you try to find your berthing, or bedroom space. While it is OK to inadvertently walk into someone's office, it is less acceptable to walk into the berthing area of the opposite sex.

Female berthing is in the same compartment with #2 Engine Space. You can get into this space from stairwells on either the port or starboard side and there is a cross hallway. Female berthing is on the port side and the door plaque clearly identifies it as Ops Berthing. Only after taking a second look at the wrinkled piece of paper taped to the door do you see that this is now Female Berthing. To add to the confusion there are two nearly identical down stairwells on the port side of the boat.

Female berthing is a narrow room with a walkway down the center and a door at each end. On the outboard side of the room are lockers and eight bunk beds. On the inner side

These top bunks are about shoulder high and there is no step for getting up. It takes practice to land in the upper bunk. Each bunk has a blue privacy curtain.

Storage under the bed keeps things from flying about during heavy seas. Coast Guard Auxilliary members often ride when the boat is going to have tours. The Auxiliarists lead tours. This is the wedge room where the narrowing hull forces the beds very close together. Notice that each bunk is equipped with an emergency breathing device in the gray and red box.

The toilets are vacuum flushed, creating a unique noise and wind as the fluid is sucked away.

of the room are more lockers, the two doors, and four bunk beds. At the end of the room is a ventilation unit.

The room certainly needs ventilation since the hanging thermometer read 82 degrees most of the time while I was there. This made the top bunks very uncomfortable and not a place for claustrophobics. The nice thing is, however, that the floor was always toasty warm, like walking on the beach. On the next deck below this berthing area are the boilers that are heating the boat. To cool off you can put your hand on a rivet in the wall. It connects directly to the out of doors and was refreshingly cold during ice breaking season.

Since crewmembers serve all types of shifts, people are coming and going at all hours and someone is sleeping almost all of the time. Talking is not allowed in berthing areas and everyone is very careful to be as quiet as possible.

All enlisted personnel sleep below the main deck where there is no natural light. Florescent lights keep the halls and rooms well lit but at night the lighting is reduced with the use of lights covered with powder blue shields. After your eyes adjust, these lights are surprisingly similar in color to morning sunshine. It is rather nice to wake up to this artificial blue sky.

The bunks are made of steel plate and are two high. Evidently, in earlier and more crowded times the bunks were canvas and three high. Even with the current configuration you cannot sit up in bed. The mattresses are thin but the beds are surprising comfortable. However, finding a place to put your glasses, watch etc. requires an intimate knowledge of the bed. It turns out that the sleeping surface is the top of an 8-in high box. Most of this box is accessed by lifting the hinged sleeping surface. There is a prop that holds it up while you store or retrieve your stuff. In the center outside edge is a small drawer that you can open and close while

lying in bed. This I discovered after several uneasy nights of wearing my glasses while asleep. Also, the bunk is not attached to the wall so things pushed against the wall fall down onto your lower bunkmate.

Storage per person includes one hanging locker where your dress uniform can be stored. Each person in female berthing also gets a drawer in addition to the under-bed box. There are a few hooks around the room and boots, shoes etc. are tucked under the bed during ice season. The beds can be further secured during rough seas by tilting them up and hooking them against the ceiling, stowed.

I had a chance to see into one of the higher ranked enlisted men's spaces and saw some personalization. One bunk, for instance had a tiny television. People had books and some had music earphones. The berthing areas were uncomfortable enough to be used nearly exclusively for sleeping.

All of the bathrooms are at the forward end of the space. You have to step through two hatches, around a stairwell and past a storage area to find the female bathroom. Across the corridor is the male bathroom with its door always open.

The bathrooms are decorated in stainless steel and vinyl. Efficiency outweighs beauty.

The toilet doors are locked when in rough seas. Every interior space has the yellow emergency light, seen in the upper left hand corner. The crewmembers all wear a small flashlight on their belts in case of a power outage.

The red sign says: "Your mother does not work here. Clean up after yourself." The female bathroom was always immaculate and never busy.

The Routine

by Sandy Planisek

The *Mackinaw* becomes home for 75 people while it is out of port. People do the same things on the *Mackinaw* that they do at home. They get up, clean up, eat breakfast, go to work, get off work, write letters, play games, exercise, go to the movies, read books, talk, and sleep. Video games and big televisions are found near most of the berthing areas.

In addition, the *Mackinaw* is a very friendly boat and almost always there are 10 or more guests riding along. Days when the captain is certain the boat will be leaving and returning to the same port become "family" days when crewmembers' families can ride along.

But it is not totally like home. You might miss the sounds of street noises, alarm clocks, and loud voices. You might also miss your privacy.

There is a shipboard work routine. The crewmembers stand watch, 4 hours of duty, and then have 8 hours off, then stand watch again in a continuous cycle. Yet every day is unique so a Plan of the Day is written and posted each morning. The big picture is outlined on the dry erase boards.

The captain is quick to mention that no plan lasts longer than 10 minutes before it is revised. Therefore, everyone stays flexible and listens to the squawk boxes.

Morning colors involves running up the flag on the stern pole.

MACKINAW'S DAILY ROUTINE

	Inport	Holiday Inport	Underway	Holiday Underway
Reveille	0600	N/A	0630	N/A
Morning Meal	0615-0645	0800-0930	0700-0800	0700-0930
Liberty Expires	0645	N/A	N/A	N/A
Workday Begins	0700	N/A	0800	N/A
Sick Call	0700-0800	N/A	0800-0900	N/A
First Call to Morning Colors	0755	0755	N/A	N/A
Morning Colors	0800	0800	N/A	N/A
Coffee Break/Request & Complaint Mast	1000	N/A	1000	N/A
Up all late Sleepers	1000	N/A	1000	N/A
Noon Meal	1300	1200-1300	1115-1200	1115-1200
Sweepers	1230	N/A	1540	N/A
Officers Call/1st Call to Quarters (optional)	1240	N/A	1210	N/A
Quarters (optional)	1245	N/A	1215	N/A
Liberty Granted/Workday Ends	1300	N/A	1600	N/A
Evening Meal	1700-1730	1700-1730	1700-1800	1700-1800
Mackinaw Cinema	N/A	N/A	1730	1730
Evening Reports	1945	1945	1945	1945
Mackinaw Cinema	N/A	N/A	2000	2000
Taps/Lights Out	2200	2200	2200	2200

Summary of changes: Updated 09/10/99
   Liberty expires at 0645 in lieu of 0700 for inport workday. Workday begins at 0700.
   Evening reports are scheduled for 1945 both inport and underway.

Casual conversation takes place on the mess deck. This just as easily might be a muster or training session.

Claudia, known as "Doc" when she is in uniform, buys t-shirts in the "exchange", a unique store that is so small that only four people are allowed inside at one time.

Tucked in by the emergency breathing tanks is an outgoing mail box. When in port the mail is exhanged.

Cell phones work in some locations, but not while out in the middle of Whitefish Bay. To get privacy the crew uses the porthole indentations on the mess deck as private phone booths. Here two crewmembers are calling home.

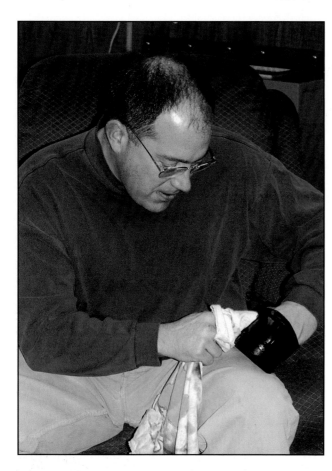

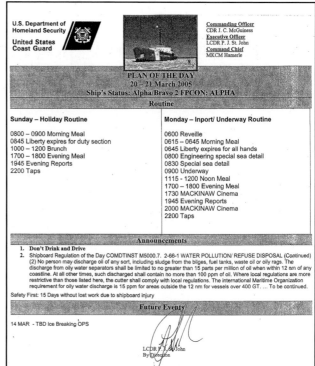

U.S. Department of
Homeland Security

United States
Coast Guard

Commanding Officer
CDR J. C. McGuiness
Executive Officer
LCDR P. J. St. John
Command Chief
MKCM Hamerle

PLAN OF THE DAY
20 – 21 March 2005
Ship's Status: Alpha/Bravo 2 FPCON: ALPHA

Routine

Sunday – Holiday Routine

0800 – 0900 Morning Meal
0845 Liberty expires for duty section
1000 – 1200 Brunch
1700 – 1800 Evening Meal
1945 Evening Reports
2200 Taps

Monday – Inport/ Underway Routine

0600 Reveille
0615 – 0645 Morning Meal
0645 Liberty expires for all hands
0800 Engineering special sea detail
0830 Special sea detail
0900 Underway
1115 - 1200 Noon Meal
1700 – 1800 Evening Meal
1730 MACKINAW Cinema
1945 Evening Reports
2000 MACKINAW Cinema
2200 Taps

Announcements

1. **Don't Drink and Drive**
2. Shipboard Regulation of the Day COMDTINST M5000.7. 2-66-1 WATER POLLUTION/ REFUSE DISPOSAL (Continued) (2) No person may discharge oil of any sort, including sludge from the bilges, fuel tanks, waste oil or oily rags. The discharge from oily water separators shall be limited to no greater than 15 parts per million of oil when within 12 nm of any coastline. At all other times, such discharged shall contain no more than 100 ppm of oil. Where local regulations are more restrictive than those listed here, the cutter shall comply with local regulations. The international Maritime Organization requirement for oily water discharge is 15 ppm for areas outside the 12 nm for vessels over 400 GT. … To be continued.

Safety First: 15 Days without lost work due to shipboard injury

Future Events

14 MAR - TBD Ice Breaking OPS

LCDR P. J. St. John
By Direction

The Plan of the Day

There are plans and schedules, but there also is the daily military routine. No one is excluded. Above, the captain is polishing his dress shoes while below an officer and enlisted man polish their boots.

There are some personal touches on the boat like the hula dancers found on the bridge.

Families Share the Mackinaw Experience

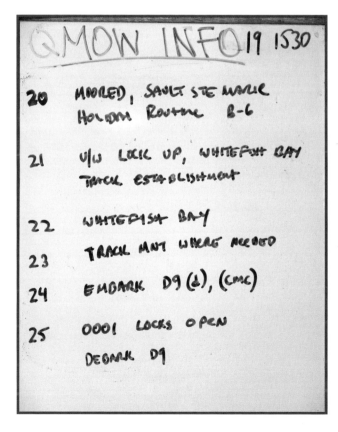

Recreation

by Master Chief Hamerle

"One of the bigger recreational activities is playing electronic games. There are Xbox games in many of the common area lounges. They are connected by cable so that somebody playing the video game down below decks can play his opponent above decks or aft. Most of them are 'shoot-them-up games'. They really enjoy killing the Master Chief. I don't' give them any slack. It is fun to hear them down below yelling, 'I got him, I got him'.

"Last night we had casino night. The first class took the opportunity to set up some gaming tables, no money involved. Any chips you won you could bid on door prizes. We have a game board Axis and Allies. My first year here chess was popular and we had a chess tournament. We have a good bit of fitness equipment. There is a small gym on the 01 deck and a bicycle outside of forward berthing. There is enough to keep occupied. A lot of reading.

"Sometimes different groups will offer to cook for the crew, and usually it is pizza night. The chiefs might do that. The cooks will help us with the dough and sauce but we will do all the topping, and baking, and serve it. It gives the cooks a break and gets us out there on the serving line feeding the deck-plate sailors. They enjoy that. We have to clean up after ourselves.

"If you compare *Mackinaw* to the other ships, she is probably the roomiest. The berthing areas for even the youngest sailors are only in 2-high racks. The chiefs all enjoy their own staterooms. In the new cutters you have two to four chiefs sharing a berthing area. We are lucky to have that privacy. In my stateroom I have my own TV and DVD player as well as room for my golf clubs."

The recreation room recently was turned into an exercise room in support of tougher fitness standards. Before this change, when this was a television room, the room was heavily used.

The Xbox games, while not pretty, serve a useful purpose.

The board game Axis and Allies is popular.

Food
Chief Terry Sorenson

by Terry Sorenson

How many people work in the galley?

"Six. There are generally three people cooking at one time. The cooks all do everything. Some are better at certain tasks than others. One guy's main job is to do the breakouts, bring the food up from storage in advance of the meal. He orders the food and does the paperwork. One person will be duty cook for the day. The duty cook gets up in the morning and cooks breakfast. Just before breakfast begins another cook will come in to help him to make sure everything goes smoothly. The duty cook changes every day on straight rotation. The duty cook is responsible to make sure the meal gets done. He will assign the other cooks a job to do. You do the soup, you do the salad bar, and I'll do the main entrée. The cooks get there at 6 in the morning and probably won't be done until 7 at night. The only watch that they stand is BMOW, bosun mate of the watch. They only stand a watch once every two days. The work is constant."

Do you have a history of past menus that have been tried?

"Yes. We have to keep them on file for three years. We have a lot of recipes. We have two great big books that we call a local recipe. That is a recipe that someone else has brought in. Then there is a book called the *Armed Forces Recipe Service*, which is the standard set of recipes that all armed forces use. I write the menus for the coming weeks.

Prime rib and baked potatoes made a special meal during icebreaking while the Admiral was aboard.

"We spend about $750 dollars a day and that serves 80 to 90 people. Right now we are loaded up for ice season. We have $51,000 worth of stores onboard.

"When we are in port and we have a lot of food onboard, we make the menus around that so we aren't using as much stuff. In port most people eat lunch and then they get liberty and go home. We cook the dinner meal but it is just for the duty section, usually 20 people or so."

Do you have a computer program that figures what you need?

"No, it is all in my head from the experience of doing it so long. If you are going to serve something in pieces, like chicken, then you know you need 80 some pieces. We cut our own steaks out of the loins. We know that we usually get 15-17 loins out of a strip.

Dry goods are stored two decks down. Carrying a day's worth of food up to the galley is work. Terry says they spend about $20,000 a month on food. For ice season they generally load $60,000 of food because they are often gone 2-3 months. While breaking ice they will load an additional $10-20,000 worth of perishable stores.

"The dry storage space is really big, a little more than we need. We have three walk-in refrigeration units. One is a freezer, one is for vegetables and produce, and one is for dairy. The day before the meal we go down to the storeroom and pick out the stuff. If it is strip loin it takes 2-3 days to thaw. We pull it out and put it into the produce box to thaw. So when the day comes that it is on the menu we have thawed meat to work with."

How do you pick what to serve?

"Last night we had veal shanks, first time we did it. It wasn't a real big hit, probably won't do it again. Every time the crew changes the tastes change. I have surveys down at the line or people come up and request something. One

The duty cook for the day gets to choose the day's music in the galley.

time somebody requested grilled peanut butter and jelly. I did it once. Will I do it again? Probably not. If they ask for it, we try it. If it goes well we keep it and do it again. If it doesn't, it is gone.

"We are very limited on serving area. We only have three steam tables. We can put stuff on the grill to keep it hot. Presentation is what sells food. I try to get the cooks to present it well. If it really looks good, people will eat it. Fish is a prime example. Joe Kraft, 2nd class, is one of the best fish cooks I have ever seen. He presents them well. They are colorful with a lot of vegetables. People who normally don't eat fish want to try it because it looks good. That is the key. I like to try to get people to eat different things. Some people grew up without a wide variety of food. They come here and they see it and say, 'I don't like that.' 'Have you ever eaten it before?' 'No.' Then try it. It is free. You might as well put one on your plate and try it. A lot of people have come back and said, 'That was really good.' All the cooks take care of the galley. They clean it after each meal. They

The cafeteria-style line is small and the crew lines up down a narrow corridor to pass by the line. They serve over a period of 30 minutes to an hour.

all wanted to cook. It is a job you have to want to do because there is always someone who is going to complain."

Are you in charge of the dirty dishes part?

"Yes. Those are mess cooks. The people who actually cook are called duty cooks. A mess cook is a non-rate, E3 or below. They are first term; they just came into the Coast Guard. They don't work for me all of the time. You have deck department and engineers. The firemen work for the engineers and the seamen work for the deck. Every month, deck is required to give me two guys and engineer is required to give me one guy for 30 days. One of them will go in the scullery where they do the dishes. One will be assigned to the mess deck where the main crew eats. He makes sure the coffee is made, the room is clean, everything is stocked, and all the tables are set up for chow. The other one is assigned to the chiefs and officers. He will set up the tables, clean the mess, clean the heads, clean the staterooms, and take out their trash. He also cleans the captain's cabin."

What is your most memorable experience?

"One of the neatest was standing on the ice under the Mackinac Bridge. During ice breaking we go through a lot more soup. Everyday at 10 am they get a break. We always have soup ready. They come in from outside or up from the engine room, which is really cold too."

What was the most unexpected thing?

"The change of schedule. Most of the other Coast Guard billets have a set schedule. They are gone for two months, home for two months, gone for two months. Simple. You get here and there are no rules, especially during ice season. You get ready to pull into port and the decision is made to turn around and head back out. Maybe one of the iron ore carriers has called up and said, 'Hey, we are stuck. We need you.' The fresh stuff is hard to plan. We only have enough space for fresh food and milk for a little over a week, two weeks max. If we are expecting to pull in and we have fresh stuff ordered and then we turn around and head out, we may run out of lettuce or stuff for the salad bar. It doesn't happen very often but once in a great while it does.

The skullery is the place dirty dishes are cleaned. New crew members serve this duty for the first month onboard.

"In home port we order supplies and Gordon Foods or Sysco brings it to the boat. If we are going to be gone for two weeks we make sure we have two weeks of menus ready. My number one problem is getting food in ice season. I have to use Gordon Food when we are in the Soo because they have a store in town. Command will tell us we are going to pull in Monday, Tuesday, or Wednesday but we aren't sure which. I'll call my rep and tell him to deliver my order to the Gordon Food store on Monday. Now it doesn't matter if

Jason and spices.

I pull in Monday, Tuesday, or Wednesday. Then we have to go to the Gordon Food store and load it into trucks and bring it over. They won't deliver from the store. We get a vehicle from the Soo Coast Guard base. A lot of times it is $10,000 worth of food. It takes three or four trips to the store."

How does this career affect your family?

"It is hard on the kids especially. Not so bad here since you are not gone so long. When I was on a 270 out of Portsmouth you are gone two months. Your wife has to be independent. As soon as I leave, the car breaks down, or the hot water heater goes, or the house floods. She is a stay-at-home mom. The beauty of the Coast Guard is that when you move, somebody else packs you. Here we have Coast Guard housing. But that is not available every place. Sometimes you have to rent a place or buy. They give you so many days to go to your next spot and many people take a couple of weeks of leave and make it vacation time. It is hardest on the kids because they don't get to keep friends.

The current stainless steel kitchen appliances were new in the 1990s. Today the entire kitchen is powered by electricity. Originally it was powered by steam from boilers.

It is hard on us because we don't get to keep friends. My wife will go for years without making friends because she hates saying good-bye.

"When I retire I want to open a hot dog cart."

It is always Taco Tuesday, Cheeseburger Wednesday, and Seafood Friday with a second choice on Friday.

Stocking the wardroom refrigerator. The officers eat in the wardroom and the chiefs eat in their own dining room. Both groups are served restaurant-style by a crewmember.

Jason cooking pizza for the crew.

Two fellows giving their dishwashing buddy a hard time. The mess deck is a place for relaxation.

by Terry Sorenson

"I wanted to run my own galley. We try to give the best food possible. Does it happen every time, no? If I'm not here, do they get lazy? Sometimes. I take a lot of pride in the food operation. If something comes out bad I will pull it off the line, even if it means pulling out hot dogs to serve. We get guys off their 4 o'clock watch and maybe things aren't going right. They sit on the mess deck to eat breakfast. It is their time to get away from things and if they get a bad meal, it makes the day worse. A good hot meal lifts a lot of spirits. That is their camaraderie time. The mess deck is definitely a meeting place, not just a place they eat.

"There are a lot of special receptions because it is the *Mackinaw*. We do those on the fantail. We serve up to 150 to 200 extra people. We did one change of command on the fantail where we served over 500 people"

Joe slicing meat.

The steam jacket kettles hold about five gallons of soup. Soup is a regular during icebreaking season.

Morale

by Sandy Planisek

Morale is a fine balance between expectation and experience. The *Mackinaw* is run with a steady hand so morale is not a major problem.

There was one occasion when you could just see the morale of the ship sinking. I could not tell you any one or two things that led me to believe a problem was developing, but even I was aware of a change. Let me set the stage.

We were returning from the Christmas Tree Ship event in Chicago. The plan was to run on to Rogers City for fuel and then stop in Cheboygan and pick up family members for a one-day "familiarization" trip up the St. Marys River before returning to Cheboygan.

The weather did not cooperate and the heavy seas forced us to anchor for most of a day just west of Bois Blanc Island, in sight of the Cheboygan River. Everywhere you looked you saw crewmembers on the phones talking to home, which was within easy sight. Although I did not hear a single person wonder aloud why we just didn't pull into port to wait out the storm, I did hear the captain explain that running into a narrow channel, like the river, with a high wind was dangerous. He also announced that the delay forced him to cancel "family day." Expectations could not be met.

Chief Sorenson has developed quick remedies to boost morale and he called out all of his tools. He, with permission of the captain and help of the senior crewmembers, announced "Casino Night." "Anyone not on duty can wear civilian clothes" was announced over the loud speaker. Chief Sorenson announced that in addition to the games there would be popcorn and ice cream for all.

"Casino Night on the Mackinaw." This event is proof that people can have lots of old-fashioned fun without money or alcohol being used.

Chief Terry Sorenson is leaning on the mixer in the back galley. His crew does most of the baking from scratch including pies, cookies, cakes, bread and pizza dough. Six or seven pies are sufficient to serve 80 crewmembers. They are not big desert eaters. Generally they cook one cake and it will last through lunch and dinner.

To my amazement, the galley crew produced a regular movie-theater-type popcorn maker. Popcorn smells started to permeate the hull and three flavors of ice cream with all of the toppings appeared. In about an hour everyone was smiling and enjoying him or herself. It was the old-fashioned party that I had not seen in years. Morale was restored.

Chief Sorenson will quickly tell anyone that the most important machine on the boat is not the engine, not the generator, not the motor; it is the coffee maker. This tool is used daily in support of the crew.

I was very impressed with the understanding that Food Service's primary mission is not to feed the crew, but to keep the crew happy. It is a major responsibility, well performed.

---

by Chief Terry Sorenson

The food is one of the biggest morale boosters on the ship. There are some things we can do for morale. We might bake scones or fresh donuts. We have soup at 10am. People spend a lot of time on the mess deck. There is not a lot of space on the boat and that is one place that people can gather, swap stories, and have a bite to eat.

Ice cream brought everyone to the mess deck.

Operations

by LT Doug Wyatt, Operations Officer

"I am the navigator for the ship. When we have an assignment the captain tells me where he wants to go, when he wants to sail, how fast he wants to get there, what speed he wants to turn for, and then I lay down the track lines. I am responsible for getting the ship from point A to point B and for making sure we have line handlers when we sail out and when we pull in. I speak with the captain at least once a day, sometimes more often. I have three junior officers who work for me. This will be their first assignment after school. Their primary duty on the *Mackinaw* is to qualify as a deck watch officer. The deck watch officer is the person on the bridge totally responsible for the safe navigation of the vessel during their 4-hour watch. They have the entire crew's lives in their hands. If they make a mistake, people could get hurt.

"When we are underway most of my time is spent up on the bridge. Before we get underway and before we moor we have a 'nav' brief so everyone knows the plan. I also have to keep an eye on the weather to make sure it is safe to transit through an area. The Great Lakes get pretty bad and icebreakers, by nature of the ship design, don't ride very well in rough seas. I am responsible for the operations side of the ship which is roughly half of the crew."

Who are the people on the bridge?

"The deck watch officer has authority over everyone on the ship except the commanding officer, the executive officer, the engineering officer and myself. The deck watch officer can tell everyone else on the ship what to do because he or she is speaking for the captain. The officer is responsible for carrying out the captain's instructions for that watch.

"There is a quartermaster of the watch, QMOW, who is laying down the fix every 15 minutes if we are in open

LT Doug Wyatt Operations Officer

Operations Department
Operations Officer

First Lieutenant	Support Officer	Navigation	Electronics
Deck work, small boats	Food Service, medical, administration	Charts and charting	Computers, satellites

---

Wyatt laying down the tracks through the St. Marys River. Planning for a trip can begin months in advance. Charts must be kept up-to-date. If the Mackinaw is going to dock, permission must be obtained from the Port Authority. Supplies must be brought aboard. Potable water tanks must be topped off and sewage tanks emptied out. All equipment must be in good operational order.

water, every six minutes if we are in the river, every three minutes if we are in restricted waters. The QMOW may take visual bearings, draw lines and tell us where we are, or take a radar fix or a GPS fix. He or she plots these fixes on the paper charts which contain the track lines for the trip. Based on where we started and how fast we are going we know how far along the track line we should be. It is called dead reckoning, or DR. We compare our fix to our DR spot on the chart and adjust our course to get back to the planned track. By monitoring these adjustments you know how the wind is affecting us. We are constantly adjusting our course based on what each fix tells us.

"There is also a bosun mate of the watch, BMOW, who makes hourly rounds of the decks to make sure everything is where it is supposed to be, everything is secure, and there are no problems. In the evening he or she also checks that all the people in the operations department are still on board, that no one has fallen overboard or gotten hurt and laying in a compartment that is not normally visited.

"There is a helmsman who is the one whose hands are actually on the wheel, steering the course.

"We have a lookout who, in decent weather, is up on the flying bridge with the big-eye binoculars and in inclement weather is in one of the conning stations. The lookout is an

A typical bridge scene. At left, looking at the radar, is the Executive Officer. He is flanked by three junior officers. In the center, under the talking tube is the helmsman and at the far end of the room is the quartermaster at the charting table.

extra set of eyes making sure that there is no one out there that is going to hit us or we are going to hit.

"Each of these positions can have a break-in person, someone learning the position, so there can be five, six, or seven people on the bridge. There is constant hands-on training."

What is the most difficult part of your job?

"Making sure I don't forget anything, little things like do we have line handlers. At 72-hours before we enter a harbor we submit what is called 'log req,' logistics request. We put in a request for line handlers from the local unit. An hour or two before we pull in to port we will call on the cell phone and confirm our arrival time and that, indeed, line handlers will be on the dock. But it is always possible that they won't be able to send handlers. Then we have to lower a small boat and send our crew ashore to catch the lines."

What is the most fun part of the job?

"Driving the ship. I am responsible for the deck watch rotation so I take at least one watch per day."

Training at the chart table is continuous. This is one of the few remaining vessels where all charting is done by hand. For the crew this is a rare opportunity to learn the old ways.

The Mackinaw is equipped with three radars units. One radar is set to a range suitable for navigation. One is set to track other vessels in the area, and the third is set for short range to monitor ice ridges.

The ship's log is kept on a computer by the quartermaster.

What is so special about this boat?

"I'm not sure. I have seen a lot of Coast Guard cutters. This is my 5th one. There is just something about this ship. No other cutter I have ever been on has had a reunion while the ship is still active. Of course I have never been on a 60-year old cutter before but, even so, this ship has a special attraction. I like that people feel this way about the ship; that is one of the reasons I asked to come to the *Mackinaw*. The entire time I have been in the Coast Guard I have been hearing about the *Mackinaw*, the Great Lakes breaker. I knew it was going to be decommissioned soon and that was part of the reason I asked to be assigned to the *Mackinaw*."

What are your fondest memories?

"Having the conn for the first time while running the Rock Cut (St. Marys River). It was the second time I had seen the Rock Cut. It is pretty narrow. Standing there watching somebody else take the ship through, 'Ah it wasn't that bad.' But when you've got the conn and you are the one telling the helmsman what to do, it appears much narrower. The goal was to get through the Rock Cut without the captain saying a word. I did it and I was proud!

"In the Rock Cut you have to worry about the two shallow water effects, bank-cushion and screw-suction. In open water you build up a plug of water in front of the hull. Bank-cushion occurs as you enter into a narrow passage. When the channel narrows, the plug of water gets bent back along side of the bow by the sidewall of the channel. This water, bouncing off the bank, tends to push the bow off to the other side. In addition, as the screw pulls water it lowers the water level between the stern of the boat and the wall. The stern is

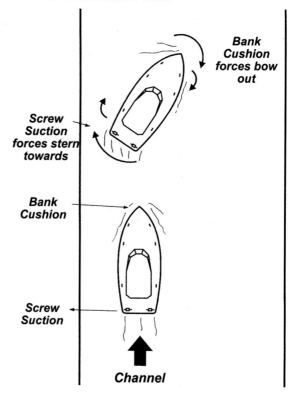

This Coast Guard instructional drawing shows the effect shallow water can have on ship maneuvering. The shallowest water that the Mackinaw has to deal with is at its home port in Cheboygan, but the Rock Cut is famous to all mariners of the Great Lakes because of its narrow channel and shallow water.

Bank Cushion forces bow out

Screw Suction forces stern towards

Bank Cushion

Screw Suction

Channel

Visibility from the bridge of the cutter is poor. A metal sprayshield just in front of the bridge windows makes it difficult to see the bow The crew has built wooden stepstools to improve forward visibility. Best visibility is from the conning towers on each side of the cutter. From these you can see forward, aft, and down alongside the hull. These were enclosed and made usable after the cutter was in service.

literally sucked towards the wall. This combination makes the ship want to turn 90 degrees in the channel. It gets your attention. You have to have a good helmsman. If you don't, you are going to have a miserable watch.

"The captain was telling me that they used to run 70 shaft-turns all the way into the jetty in Cheboygan. The bank-cushion and screw-suction would mess them up so much that they would have the rudder 20 degrees over trying to hold a steady course. That is too fast for the shallow water. You must go slower to get control. Of course it makes for a lot longer transit.

"Every time we are turning in restricted waters either the captain, the XO, or I will be there as a coach. In open water one person has both the deck and the conn because there is not that much going on. In restricted water you usually split these tasks between two people. One person has the conn, the throttles, one person has the deck. This way one person isn't overloaded. The coach is standing there keeping an eye on everything. It is real easy to get focused in on one thing and 'lose the bubble.' That means you are so focused on one aspect of the work that you lose track of the overall situation. The coach always watches the overall situation."

On smaller Coast Guard vessels the line handlers jump onto the dock as the boat approaches, but the Mackinaw requires much more planning. These dockside crew members have to be positioned in advance. As the Mackinaw approaches Cheboygan it lowers its inflatable boat with a crew. They speed ahead and get positioned on the dock before the Mackinaw lumbers in.

U.S. Coast Guard

The Rock Cut is on the west side of Neebish Island and is a 1-way, downbound, passage for freighters. This aerial photo shows the Mackinaw in front of the Edgar B. Speer as it was working to break it free of the Rock Cut. On the lower part of this picture you can actually see the walls of the Rock Cut. It is a man-made channel in the St. Marys River blasted out of solid rock. Its profile is a perfect rectangle which is 300 feet wide and 23 feet deep. The Mackinaw draws 19 feet of water and freighters often draw 21 feet, so shallow water effects occur when steering through this passage.

The Bridge

When underway, the bridge of the ship is the brain. It acts as the boat's eyes and ears. All information about the environment and internal systems is routed here for processing. For safety reasons there are redundancies in personnel, several people are watching, several people are thinking, several people are listening. And, of course, the result of this process is the need to communicate with others on board and on nearby vessels. Surveillance and communication equipment decorate the bulkheads of the bridge. The numerous people fit in around the gear.

When the boat is safely docked, the bridge rests. A vacuum seems to suck the crew out to other kinds of work, mostly paperwork done at desks tucked all over the ship. Nobody remains on the bridge unless a public tour is coming through to inspect the view from this elevated platform.

The ship's whistles are brass. The crew tests these whistles every day at noon and is careful not to touch the brass levers so they do not tarnish.

AIS system which identifies the name, cargo, and destination of all ships in the vicinity.

Radar

Radio

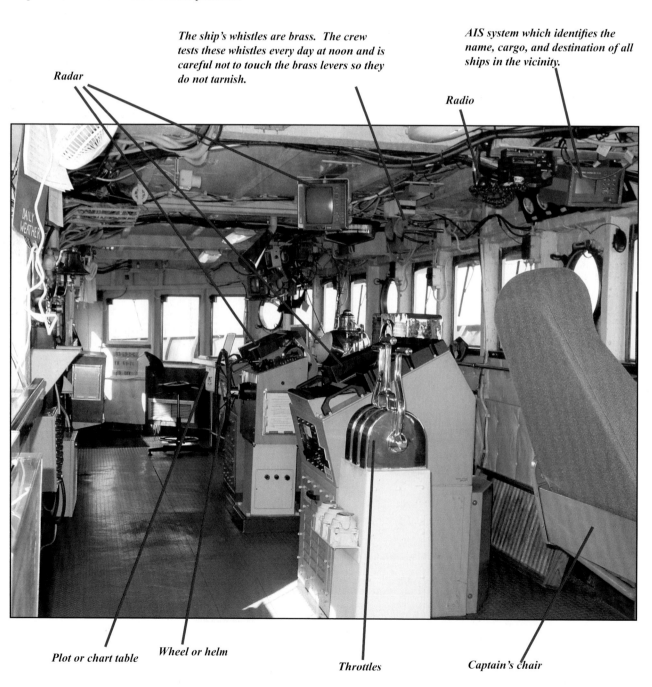

Plot or chart table

Wheel or helm

Throttles

Captain's chair

Port Side of Bridge

When looking at the bridge from the other end you can see the array of communication equipment on the back wall. While underway, the bridge and motor room are in constant communication.

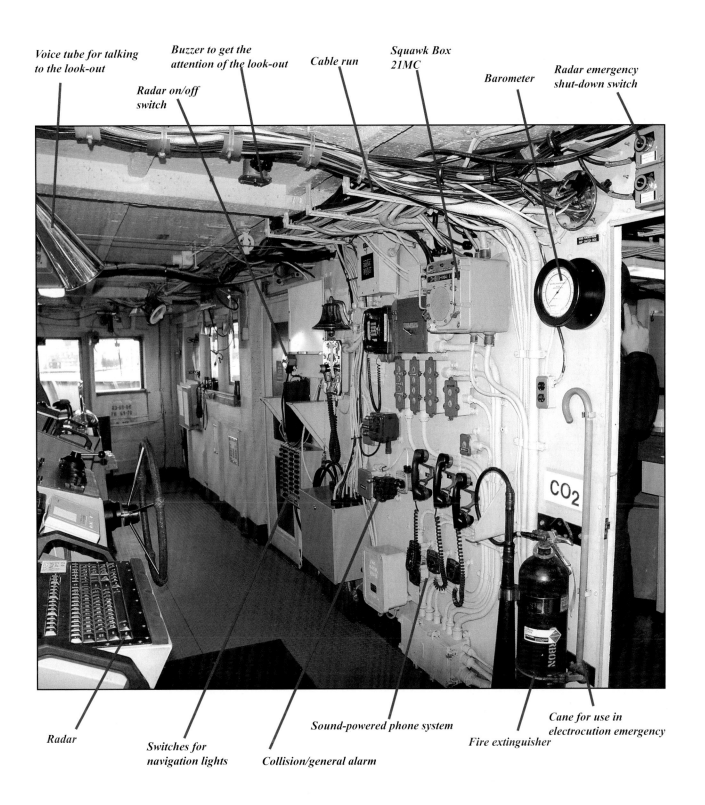

Voice tube for talking to the look-out

Radar on/off switch

Buzzer to get the attention of the look-out

Cable run

Squawk Box 21MC

Barometer

Radar emergency shut-down switch

Radar

Switches for navigation lights

Collision/general alarm

Sound-powered phone system

Fire extinguisher

Cane for use in electrocution emergency

Communication Equipment on the Bridge

Primary communication center including things like plant configuration, time of sunset, weather conditions, water levels in lake

Microphone for 1MC or ship's intercom

Ship's bell

Bridge emergency phone has its own phone number and its own distinct sound

Ship's moored / unmoored whistle

Ice breakdown light switch for the red light on the HIVAC structure and mast. To be flipped if Mackinaw becomes beset (stuck) while conducting an escort.

General emergency alarm

Collision alarm

Collision instructions

The Compass

by Sandy Planisek

The helmsman looks at two compasses; the magnetic compass and the gyrocompass repeater. The gyrocompass is in the IC Gyrospace and there are several repeaters around the ship.

The magnetic compass points to magnetic north. This direction varies from true north by as much as 20 degrees depending where on the earth you are taking the reading. This is called the compass' "variation". The magnetic compass is also affected by the ship's electrical devices and by the steel of the hull. These onboard problems are called "deviation". The big red and green iron balls are used to adjust the compass. The major advantage of the magnetic compass is that it is powered by the magnetic pull of the earth and does not rely on shipboard electrical systems.

A gyrocompass works differently than a magnetic compass. It reads true magntic north. The earth spins on its axis and the gyrocompass, using a gimbals system, will seek out this axis of rotation and read true north. The gyrocompass is powered by electricity. It must be activated for 24 hours for it to settle down and point exactly true north. Generally it is never turned off in order to maintain ship readiness. This particular gyrocompass probably came onboard in the 1960s. Even some of the new Coast Guard boats are getting this type of gyrocompass.

The bridge crew routinely uses the gyrocompass and only reverts to the magnetic compass during an electrical failure or for a reliability test.

*Inclinometer tells
the roll of the ship*

Gyrocompass repeater

Magnetic compass

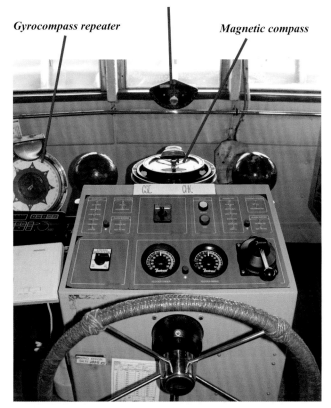

Every year Mackinaw "swings" the magnetic compass. Swinging involves determining compass directions from the location of the sun and then adjusting the red and green iron balls plus smaller magnets until the compass reads as accurately as possible. A magnetic compass is affected by both the steel in the ship's hull and the ship's electric current.

The gyrocompass reads the spin of the earth rather than using magnetism. It is more accurate but it must be turned on 24 hours before departure to assure that it has settled into an accurate reading. The main unit is on the main deck but repeaters are found in all steering locations.

Mackinaw

John Wagner

The white Mackinaw leads the Enerchem Catalyst on a curving path towards the Mackinac Bridge. Chief Hamerle noted during his interview that if you ever were standing on the back deck of the Mackinaw when the collision alarm was sounded you would understand the importance of painting the Mackinaw red. This photo shows how the white hull blended into the ice.

Navigation
BM1 Hiatt

by BM1 Mike Hiatt

"I am the bridge supervisor, Navigation Division supervisor. I work directly for the Ops boss and a Nav ensign.

"My duties for getting underway are to make sure all of the charts are prepped. Today we are planning to go to Toledo, Cleveland, Detroit, and Sarnia. I started about two weeks in advance prepping the charts to make sure they are ready for the operations officer to sign and for the captain to sign and approve. We make sure that the ship is always navigating safely."

What do you do to prep a chart?

"We have to order the charts. Once we get the chart we have to gazetteer it for our specifications. 'Gazetteer it' means highlight the shoal water, which is different for us than for another ship because of our draft. Then we put certain landmarks on there and then put courses in, courses that the captain thinks will be safe. We permanently mark our courses and we put tape over them so they don't get destroyed, whitened-out or erased."

What are the navigation tools?

"In today's world people can use a computer to navigate by. But this ship, being so old, we are not outfitted with those state-of-the-art computers. So we still use our paper charts to navigate by. We use an electronic charting system as a back up but by law we can't use that as our primary navigation tool. We use a chart, a set of dividers, a Weems,

BM1 Michael Hiatt is planning the Mackinaw's last goodwill visits. BM stands for bosun mate.

Historic navigation tools. A Weems is a set of parallel straight edges. Notice the orange, yellow and blue gazetteer marks.

and a pencil. We are using some basic tools, some basic math. This is how we are navigating. There are probably 20 ships left in the Coast Guard that have to do it this way. On the new *Mackinaw* they practice this but they don't use it every day. We do.

"When we get underway we will have four people at our plot table. One will be the evaluator. He is watching the overall plot team to make sure things are going smoothly. He is passing information over to the deck watch officer. The next person is the guy plotting. He is the guy actually working with the chart. He is using his head at all times doing a lot of math, quickly too. Then we have a guy on the nav radar. We use our radar to navigate by too. He is picking out points and doing measurements. And then we have a person doing our logs, which is the QMOW, quartermaster of the watch. They

The "nav brief" is an important communication tool used at the outset of each operation. The "nav" room is tiny and 10 or more people squeeze in to hear the deck watch officer outline the goals and assignments for the next activity. The leader of the briefing stands at the left end of the wooden table. Everyone else stands as close as possible in order to hear. There are no raised voices on the Mackinaw.

At the right edge of this photo of the chart room is a repeater radar set. Radar had only been in existence for two years when the Mackinaw was designed. The Mackinaw was one of the earliest vessels to carry radar.

are also responsible for raising and lowering the flag.

"The QMOW is in charge of the plot team. He is also in charge of the helmsman. And he is in charge of the lookout to make sure they are doing their job. The QMOW reports directly to the deck watch officer.

"If we are underway in open waters the deck watch officer is usually one person. If we are in river watch, in restricted waters or a tight area, like going down the Detroit River, St. Clair River or St. Marys River, we will have two deck watch officers up here. One navigates the ship, the conning officer, and one watches the ship itself to make sure everything is going smoothly."

How do you plan out the duties of these people?

"We usually have a navigation brief. We try to have it 24 hours prior to an evolution but usually we have it an hour before the evolution because of time restrictions. We might do 20 evolutions in a day and we don't know what those are 24 hours prior. We get the whole team together, not just the plot team, but the entire bridge team - deck watch officers, the XO, the operations officer, the plot team - everybody that is going to be up here. We go to the chart room and

do a navigation brief. We discuss everybody's position and what they are going to be doing and how it is going to go. We discuss the risk involved and we try to reduce the risks. If we think the risk is really great and we were planning on six-minute fixes, we might need to go to three minute fixes to reduce the risk. Or we might change who is doing what. If someone is a junior member and not really experienced we might get a more experienced person. Even with the deck watch officer, there are more experienced deck watch officers

Lookout with the big -eye

than others. If it is really windy outside we might get a more experienced deck watch officer to drive. If it is extremely windy the CO might even drive the ship just because of the risk involved."

What is an evolution?

"Anything with risk in it. Pulling into a port, anchoring, if we are going to enter a river, if we are going to have another cutter pulling into our notch, if we are going to be towing somebody, anything that is going to involve some risk we need to plan for. If you don't plan for it, a bad situation can happen. Whenever we have a navigation brief we always have one engineer come up here so they know what is going on in order to relay to the rest of the engineering department. They tell us the plant status, what engines we are going to have, and the draft of the ship. The captain might say he wants us to draft a certain depth. The engineering crew controls the draft of the ship."

Who runs the nav brief?

"Usually it is the deck watch officer who gives the navigation brief. They usually bring their plan to the navigation officer and say this is what I am planning. If he needs to make some changes, he will.

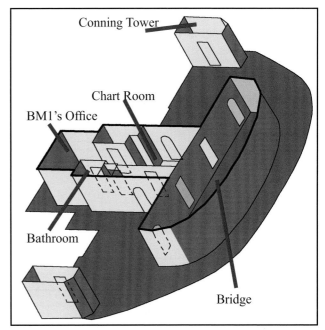

The bridge is on the 03 level, three floors above the main deck. The additions to the bridge are shaded pink. These were added early in the ship's life when it was realized that the bridge crew could not see out to the back. This is particularly important in Cheboygan where the crew navigates the river by watching the lighthouse range lights.

BM1 Hiatt at the chart box. Notice that behind him the mast of the ship passes through his office.

"On most ships there are two rooms, the bridge and the chart room. We primarily use our chart room just to prep our charts and hold our navigation briefs. The navigation division works back there. That is the workspace of the bridge where we keep all of our publications and update the charts. Back in the old days that was where they did the chart work because the bridge of the *Mackinaw* used to be a lot smaller. They prefer to chart on the bridge so they can talk back and forth to the deck watch officer. Back when the bridge was small you couldn't have a humongous chart table. An extra set of eyes is good. The deck watch officer might get focused in on one thing. If he has a ship he is approaching and he is trying to decide how that might work out, he might get so focused in on that that he is not seeing something else. The extra set of eyes helps.

"We always have a lookout up on the flying bridge above us. In the wintertime he or she works in the conning stations if it is super cold. There is a pair of binoculars up there that are 10 times as powerful as what regular binoculars are. They are called our big-eyes. The lookout is up there with those big-eyes watching out for shipping, airplanes; you name it - they are looking for it. The lookout can also see down at the water line. They have a lot better perspective up there.

"We have known about today's trip for two months. We started really planning for it about a month and a half ago, calling each port, and setting up arrangements. Usually I do that or Operations, Mr. Wyatt, does it. We call the port to make sure we have berthing. We will look at the chart and at the latest Army Corp of Engineers depth soundings and make sure our cutter will actually fit in there. Sometimes the depth of water is not good for us so we may not be able to go to that port. Two weeks out we start on our charts. We work in the chart room. We have a chart box filled with charts. All of these charts are gazetteered. I have signed them, the operations boss has signed them, and the captain has signed them. We have charts of everything from Buffalo all the way up into Lake Superior and down to Chicago.

"At the navigation brief we go through the GAR risk assessment for every operation. We rate the degree of risk from 1 to 5: 1 being slight, 5 being very high. We rate the evolution's supervision, planning, selection (qualified personnel), fitness (is the crew ready physically and mentally), environment (windy), and complexity We

At the end of each nav briefing the deck watch officer asks those at the table to rate several characteristics of the maneuver or evolution. The scores are summed and the total is compared with the scale across the bottom. If the evolution ends up with a high score, in the red, then the maneuver is reconsidered.

add up the scores and if the total gets into the red we are probably going to stop and reevaluate. If it is in green, it is acceptable. If it is in yellow, attention is required. The person giving the navigation brief will pick different people to rate the categories to get an overall view of what the entire room is thinking. If one person thinks it is a one and another person thinks it is a five, you go with the highest number. If something changes, this is not set in stone. We may say we need to stop and reevaluate. Slow and steady wins the race."

Each conning tower has a complete set of duplicate controls except for the wheel. On the very left of this photo is a spotting compass on a gyro repeater. A joy stick rudder controller also is located in the conning tower but it has been disconnected because people were bumping into it. An intercom connects the people in the conning tower with the helmsman.

Many of the electronic devices on the bridge are hooked to antennae on the mast which require maintenance. The mast is 105 feet tall.

When standing at the wheel and looking out you can just see the top of the steerng pole on the bow of the boat. Mostly you see the inside of the spray shield. You have no ability to see any vessels that may be close to the boat.

Baltimore

At the time this book was being prepared the future of the *Mackinaw* was unclear. Would it become a museum or would it be sent to the Coast Guard's yard in Baltimore?

The boat was originally designed to be wide enough that it could not leave the Great Lakes as a way of assuring it would always be used on the Great Lakes. But over the years the Saint Lawrence Seaway system has been widened. Now the only thing keeping the boat in the Great Lakes is its need for fresh lake water for cooling. The boat can go to Baltimore but the salt water it will use will cause fatal rusting.

BM1 Hiatt is in charge of preparing the charts to Baltimore. Here is what he had to say.

"The Baltimore trip comprises about 300 charts. It will take about a month and a half to get those charts ready. We have been working on that trip for about three months now. Even for our electronic charting system we will have to buy charts that will cost us from $4-10,000. We hope that doesn't happen. For the Baltimore trip we will have to use both chart tables so we can get double the amount of work done."

Above the plotting table is an array of electronics including radios, GPS, LORAN-C, a direction finder for search and rescue, an encrypting radio, and a Fathometer to tell the water depth. The red lights are to preserve the crew's night vision.

The Helm

by BM1 Hiatt

"There are three different radars running at all times on the ship. We have navigation radar for the QMOW. The other big radar is the shipping radar. We track ships with that; see if there is any traffic out there. In the ice season we use it to look for ice ridges or to see where the ice edge is. Ice comes up real nice on the radar. The other radar we have is the small radar and it can look out pretty far and see if there is shipping out there. If one person was doing the navigation, looking for shipping and looking for ice ridges all at the same time, the responsibility could be overwhelming."

What is the name of the person who stands at the helm and what are they thinking about and doing?

"The helmsman stands here or a master helmsman. The master helmsman is a more experienced helmsman who knows how to drive in ice and knows how the ship feels. The helmsman is a junior helmsman and he can drive the ship in open waters. He is taking helm commands from the deck watch officer and steering. He is also passing information to the QMOW for navigational purposes and logs.

"There are two ways he can drive. He or she can drive with the seaman's eye. The conning officer might tell the helmsman to steer on that lighthouse, or that tip of land, or maybe a giant pine tree. So he can use the seaman's eye to look out. Next he might be given a gyrocompass course to steer. He will look at the gyro repeater the whole time. He may look up every once and a while to see if he is straight but he is usually steering by the gyrocompass. If we lost our gyrocompass he can steer by magnetic compass. QMOW's correct for that. He is thinking about how the ship is moving back and forth. You can watch the water and see how the ship is moving through the water. If he is pulling to the left or pulling to the right the deck watch officer will tell him to 'mind his helm'. If the deck watch officer wants him to turn to the right he might say 'right standard rudder' which is right 20 degrees rudder or he could say 'come right to a course of 042'."

I see them spin the wheel. How much do they spin it?

"It depends on how fast the deck watch officer wants them to come around to that course. If the deck watch officer (DWO) just tells him a course, DWO is worried where the ship is going but not about how fast it is going to get around to that. Some helmsmen are really slow going there and some of them spin the wheel really quickly. We want them to move it slowly. The rudder doesn't move any faster by spinning the wheel faster. If there is a really big course change the deck watch officer might say 'right 20 degree rudder'. The deck watch officers study that and know how the ship will turn at a certain speed. We know when to 'turn on a turn' (begin the turning process). DWO might tell them rudder amidships and he might tell them to 'meet her,' which tells them to steady up the ship, which might be swinging. Then DWO tells them to 'mark their head'. They will look at the gyrocompass and they will read out the heading. Then DWO might say 'steady up on course'. The helmsman can steer by the traditional wheel or he can steer by the joystick.

"We have a backup for the bridge steering system. We can also steer the ship down in aft steering a couple of different ways. We can do it manually with a wheel down there. It takes 120 revolutions on that wheel to turn the ship one degree. It takes all of the junior members of the ship to take turns forcing that wheel. We also have a hydraulic winch system down there to turn the ship. We go down there and practice in case we lose steering on the bridge

"There is also a rudder angle indicator above the helmsman. That lets the deck watch officer know what the rudder is doing. That is a tattletale that lets everyone make sure the helmsman is doing his job."

What is the worst worry in their mind?

"If we are driving in ice the deck watch officer likes the ship to be in a straight line. But there are ice ridges that push the ship off of that straight line. Or you might hit some very heavy ice and the ship wants to track back and forth to find the best way through the ice. That is probably the most stressful time for the helmsman. Or if we are diving through a really tight river, like the St. Marys River or the St. Clair River or Detroit River, they want to make sure they are doing their job. If the deck watch officers are stressed, that puts a little stress on the helmsman."

The helmsman is steering with seaman's eyes.

The Helm

Bridge

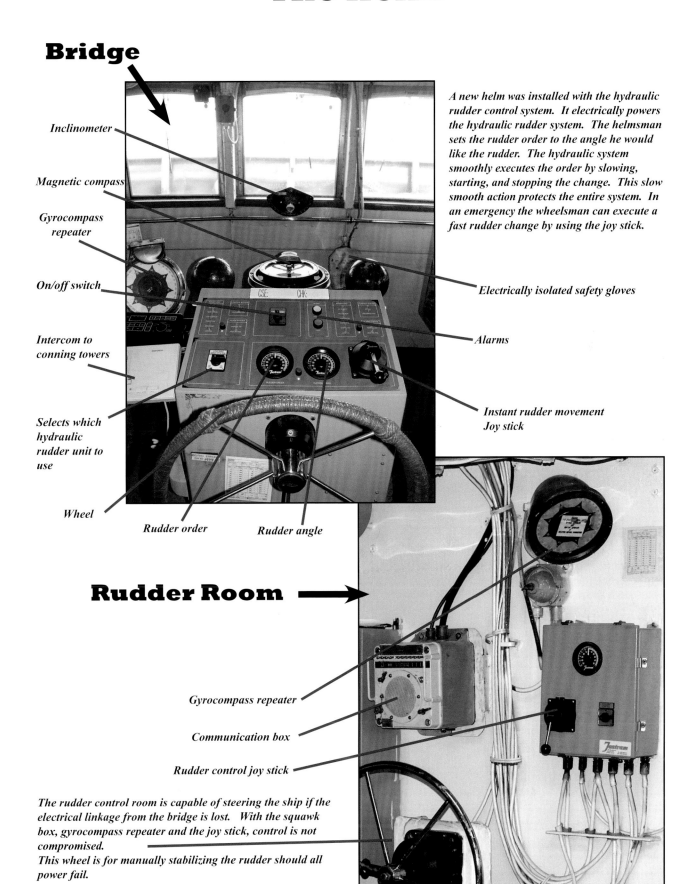

Inclinometer

Magnetic compass

Gyrocompass repeater

On/off switch

Intercom to conning towers

Selects which hydraulic rudder unit to use

Wheel

Rudder order

Rudder angle

A new helm was installed with the hydraulic rudder control system. It electrically powers the hydraulic rudder system. The helmsman sets the rudder order to the angle he would like the rudder. The hydraulic system smoothly executes the order by slowing, starting, and stopping the change. This slow smooth action protects the entire system. In an emergency the wheelsman can execute a fast rudder change by using the joy stick.

Electrically isolated safety gloves

Alarms

Instant rudder movement Joy stick

Rudder Room ➡

Gyrocompass repeater

Communication box

Rudder control joy stick

The rudder control room is capable of steering the ship if the electrical linkage from the bridge is lost. With the squawk box, gyrocompass repeater and the joy stick, control is not compromised.
This wheel is for manually stabilizing the rudder should all power fail.

Speeding Up

by Sandy Planisek

April 2006

I have spent 18 months visiting, living, and talking on the *Mackinaw*. I can now approach the ship confident that I can walk up the brow without tripping on the little ridges, I can open the door without too much thought, and can even find some of the spaces and people inside the ship. A few questions about details here and there and I will be able to finish writing this book.

With this confidence I very casually asked, "What happens when you want the boat to go faster and you push the throttles forward?" Of course I expected an answer like, "it engages an electric motor." The answer I got was not even close.

Air pressure and bicycle chains make the ship go faster. I have heard the boat affectionately called the CGC MacGyver. I couldn't wait to hear this story.

MK1 Mike Backlas first told me this story. Then EM1 Nate Koupal told me again and offered to show me the air and bicycles, but he was called away. Here is the story I heard, which can sometimes be different from what was said.

When the helmsman pushes the throttles he activates a physical linkage in the "Helter Skelter." I might digress one

The red, yellow, and green lights indicate that these throttles are in neutral, the engines are not engaged. The person running the throttles can be the "conn" or the less experienced "lee helmsman."

EM1 Nate Koupal is explaining the throttles and showing me the original manuals for the engines and towing winch in the engineering work room. This is a tiny, low ceiling space with a cage holding tools, fititngs and manuals.

moment to say that the "Helter Skelter" is a space under the captain's quarters that everyone said to stay away from. It was described as a knee-high space strung with wires running to and from the bridge, like a pot of spaghetti with wires everywhere running helter skelter. Enter at your own risk on your belly and worry about being electrocuted. With that description, I had never asked to see it.

But, it was explained, the throttle linkages turned into bicycle chains and sprockets in the Helter Skelter. These abbreviated bicycles turn vernier gauges that somehow create air pressure that ultimately causes the propellers, 165 feet away, to turn faster. I thought I was having a massive mental meltdown trying to understand this. Then I asked a third person, LTJG Andy Lawrence, who explained it again.

The throttles on the bridge create air pressure that goes to the vernier gauges mounted on the motor room switchboard. From there, the air pressure goes to the governors on the engines. More air pressure causes the governors to supply more fuel and that creates more speed in the engines. Faster engines create faster generators that create faster propulsion motors, shafts, and propellers. Nothing to it. And most interesting the linkage from the throttles to the air is by bicycle chains. Andy asked if I wanted to see them.

Of course I did as long as I didn't have to enter the death defying Helter Skelter. No problem, you can just peer in the door. So I did.

Not everyone likes to get green hands at the throttles. So the throttles get cleaned regularly.

Here is the view through the doorway of Helter Skelter. Directly inside the door are the startling bicycle parts. Each of the three throttles controls three chains, one to each motor space. The notorious wire maze is on the other side of the far perforated wall.

The Throttles

by Mike Hiatt

"Traditionally these are called throttles on a boat. But this is also called our 'lee helm.' The lee helmsman is usually another deck watch officer.

"An experienced deck watch officer can drive the ship from here without the benefit of any rudder movement. These throttles are operated with air. When you push the throttle forward it shoots air down to the control in the motor rooms. It tells the engines what to do. It is usually the deck watch officer that is running these himself. Every once and a while we have a lee helmsman. When we go through the locks we have a lee helmsman. The deck watch officer might say, '30 turns', which is 30 rmps of the propeller. He might say, '30 turns ahead on the port shaft. 20 turns astern on the starboard shaft. 20 turns ahead on the bow shaft.' We have a bow shaft, which most vessels don't have anymore. They are going to azipods or bow thrusters. Our bow prop is unique.

"This is nice because if you put the bow shaft 30 turns ahead, it wants to pull you almost like a bow thruster. So all you have to do is push the bow shaft ahead and port back and it spins the ship in a perfect little circle right there. It will turn on a dime. Traditionally most people didn't use the bow shaft. But the captain we have today likes to use this. It is a tool; why not use it to our best advantage? If we are pulling into port or out of port it will get us away from the dock easier. We just walk ourselves out like a traditional bow thruster does. Also it will help us go through the ice a little bit easier, it lubricates the hull by sending a flow of water along the sides. It keeps ice out of the sea strainers. It helps us."

Do you have to keep the revolutions on the bow prop higher than the aft props?

"We have an amp gauge up here (The black box and dials above Mike's head on the next two photos). We don't want to 'over amp' the engines. So we try to keep them at max amps in ice. It is really a chore to keep the engines balanced. If you hit a heavy piece of ice they want to rev up. Too many amps make the engines trip off line. You don't want that, especially if you have a 1,000-foot freighter behind you. You don't want it to ram into the back of you. We have three sets of throttles: one set on the bridge and a set in each conning station. When we are coming close to something we go to the nearest conning station to control the ship and the captain is always there giving us advice.

"This is our amp and rpm gauge. It will tell our rpms for each propeller. It also tells our amps for each motor. We have a chart of max amps for each shaft. You also watch the air control. If we do 30 turns on the two aft shafts we are doing about 3 knots. If we do 75 turns we are doing 10 knots. If we do 105 turns we are doing about 13 knots. We can do 14 to 15 knots if we really push it. When we come into the river we might do 3 knots or a little less. We are trying to ease it in. Slow is safe.

"Down here are our engine alarms. If we over amp they trip themselves off line so it doesn't damage the diesels. The yellow light says we have tripped a shaft. That is the conning officer or deck watch officer's fault. We over ran the ship. It will give a big buzzing sound and a yellow light. If we get a yellow light we get right on the phone to the main control. They tell us the estimated time of getting the problem fixed. It can take from maybe 10 minutes to an hour if we overheat. If we are only running two engines they can just put another engine into the loop almost immediately.

Chadburn or engine order telegraph   *air pressure and amp gauge*

"We have an engine order telegraph. Most ships don't have these anymore. It is an extra set of throttles and we can use it as an extra helm. We do test it and practice using it."

"This is very stressful if you are in the river breaking ice and you have a freighter behind you and you have an engine alarm go off. You get worried really quick if you are the conning officer. Something has really gone wrong.

"This past fall we were up in the St. Marys River training and the entire ship went dark while we were in a tight channel. Most people were wondering what was going on. Automatically the captain, being the captain, took total control. When we are in the river we have an anchor ready to drop. We dropped it right there. He calmed everybody down and found out what the problem was. They fixed the

problem and we were back underway in about an hour. If we go "dark ship" we flip the switch on the red light on the back deck. The freighter behind us then knows we are going to stop; therefore, they are going to have to stop. A few years ago a ship did run into the *Mackinaw*. We have battery back-ups for the bridge that last about 30 minutes.

"It takes about two years to get the total feel of how the cutter operates. Some of the older guys come and they just know how to make the ship move. Like the captain, he is one of the best at it. He can really move the throttles around and make the ship move how he wants it to."

Air, amps and revolutions

by Sandy Planisek

Turns, amps, air are all monitored by the deck watch officer on the bridge. "Turns" are revolutions per minute of the propellers. "Amps" are the amount of electrical power applied to the propeller shafts. "Air" regulates the power applied to the engines.

Why do the bridge personnel use these different and confusing ways to talk about controlling the speed of the boat? It has to do with whether the boat is cruising or working, whether speed is more important or power.

When just cruising along, the boat travels through water that varies little in density. Under these conditions there is a direct correlation between the air pressure sent from the helm, the amps on the motors, and the revolutions on the props. Using one scale is equivalent to using another. Perhaps the easiest to understand is turns. Thirty turns is slow speed used for entering the Cheboygan River and other narrow passages. Seventy turns is medium speed for wide channels. One hundred and twenty turns is fast speed used to make progress while traveling down the unobstructed center of the lakes.

Things get complicated during ice breaking when the three scales may not directly correlate because the boat is traveling through ice, slush, snow, and water. These stages of water cause different resistance and pressure on the props. In this scenario the turns become secondary and the amount of power used is of prime importance. There is always the desire to have more power so amps must be monitored.

The boat is self-protecting, and if the bridge asks for too many amps, the engines can and will shut down. There is nothing worse than overshooting the amps to discover that you have totally killed the power.

Too much air pressure and too many turns can also kill the engines. That happened many years ago on Lake Erie during the attempt to break out a freighter. When the towing cable which was holding the *Mackinaw* broke, the *Mackinaw* moved freely ahead. The throttleman, in an attempt to slow the boat, slammed back the throttles and all of the starboard engines shut down. This creates a steering problem and, of course, a risky situation. It takes about a minute to get the engines back on line but that minute can seem very long.

Clearly, a good deck watch officer keeps a constant eye on all three sets of gauges and moves the throttles in a slow and easy manner.

Air pressure   *RPMs*   *Amps*

The Bow Prop

by LTJG Molly Killen

"The day we were transiting the very narrow channel into Green Bay to make sure it was open for shipping, the ice was very heavy. We were having some problems with our sea chest icing up so we engaged our bow prop. That largely eliminated the sea chest icing by sending that extra stream of water back along the hull. That is important because we draw cooling water through the sea chests. If they are blocked by ice our engines will overheat. So, ironically, ice causes our engines to overheat, which means you have to shut the engines down. If we lose our 'way' through the ice we can lose a lot of momentum. We stand the risk of becoming beset ourselves or of having to go back and ram the ice, which is not good for the plant or the ship. It is better to keep moving at a steady pace.

"So we used our bow prop and we were running at approximately 100 turns with our port and starboard shafts and maybe 70 or 80 turns with our bow prop. The helmsman actually had to 'keep on right 10 degrees rudder' to keep the ship moving on the course we wanted. The reason for that is our bow prop exerts torque on the ship to the point that it will pull us off to the left. There is denser water deeper down than higher up so the bottom of the bow screw's rotation is going to exert more torque than it does at the top.

"As we were coming into the channel the ice was gradually beginning to lighten up so we gently brought down the speed of the bow prop. The conning officer and helmsman maintained close communication. As we took the bow prop off we gradually took the rudder off (straightened it). We took it slow and kept the communication between the conning officer and helmsman running smoothly. Gradually we worked it off until the rudder amidships was actually keeping the ship on course.

"We can use the bow shaft with the starboard shaft to pull ourselves into the pier sidewise. Our bow does hang over the pier a little bit. So another reason for using the bow prop, besides showing off for the crowd, is that if there are a lot of objects on the pier that we risk crushing when we are coming in at a steep angle, we can just move the boat straight in sideways using the bow and starboard shafts and our wires. That will mitigate a lot of risk as well."

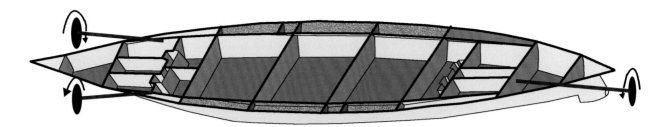

When placed in forward the top blades on the stern props are moving outward. The bow prop moves like the port prop, counterclockwise when looking at it from the bridge.

by Sandy Planisek

Captain McGuiness is a born teacher. At lunch one day I asked how the *Mackinaw* could move sideways to a dock using its bow prop and I drew the drawing to the right. His immediate response was, "It cannot."

"But," I stammered, "I thought . . ."

He was drawing a new sketch. He started to explain.

"You have to remember that the bow prop is only 12 feet in diameter and the stern props are 14 feet. Since the tips do all of the work, that diameter difference makes a significant difference in power. Also you need to remember that propellers are curved blades, designed to create power when moving forward. Reverse is possible but it is very inefficient. Given these two constraints it would be exceedingly difficult to get the boat to move parallel to a dock on its right.

"What we can do is make the boat move sideways to a dock on its port side (left). Here is why. If we put the bow prop on forward it will tend to pull the bow of the

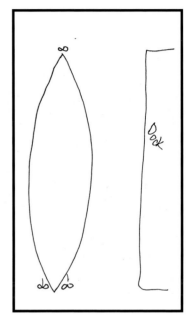

boat to the left. This he indicated with the #1 curve on the drawing. The starboard rear prop spins in the opposite direction of the bow prop, #2. So if we put it into reverse it will spin the same direction as the bow prop and also push the stern toward the dock.

"This combination of the small bow prop moving forward in its most powerful direction and the starboard stern prop moving in its weakest direction, reverse, creates balanced pressures on the front and back of the boat. The boat moves in parallel to the dock. It works great."

Then he drew the resulting force drawing.

"But if we try to do the same thing with a starboard tie (to the right) it does not work because the small bow prop would have to be in reverse thus weakening it further, and the larger stern prop would be in forward and thus significantly overpowering the bow.

"Understanding this balance allows us to do interesting things."

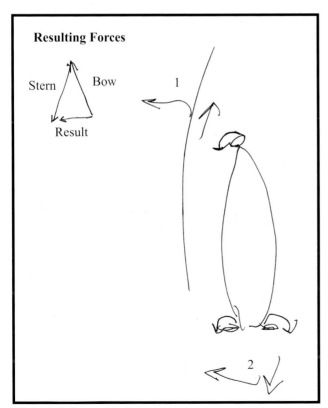

CDR McGuiness' sketch.

Chris Winters

This dramatic photo of the a fish-eye view of the bow prop was taken while the Mackinaw was in dry dock for repairs. Notice that the edge of the bow prop shows some wear.

Support Officer
LTJG Molly Killen

by LTJG Molly Killen

"I am LTJG Molly Killen.

"The main driving force behind this, my office, is the fact that I am not married, have no children, and my job comprises the largest portion of my life right now. I spend a great deal of time aboard the ship even though I do have a house, so I want to make this room as comfortable as possible. I want it to be a safe haven to return to after a hectic day of work. I also want to make it seaworthy. I tried to secure everything in a seaman like fashion. I've got my Christmas lights up because it lends a really warm glow to the place. And I want it to be a productive work environment at the same time. I spend long periods of time doing administration that goes along with my job as a department head.

"My primary duty is deck watch officer, driving the ship, and my primary collateral duty is support department officer. I am in charge of the cooks, our corpsman, our yeoman, and our storekeepers".

Can you explain how information flows down and back up?

"The captain is the link between the group at District and *Mackinaw* and her missions, so he deals at the cutter level and up. XO deals at the cutter level and down. The captain and XO really act as a leadership team. They work very well

The Eagle

The Eagle

together, as a captain and executive officer should. They are the ones that work with the long-range plan for *Mackinaw*. They are the ones that give us the order of what we are going to do on a weekly, monthly, and yearly basis. Their orders come from the district level, who decides where *Mackinaw* is most needed right now. They execute those orders through the department heads. We have LCDR Barner who is our engineer officer in charge of the engineering department, and then we have LT Wyatt who is our operations officer in charge of operations department.

"The Operations Department is further broken down into the Deck Department or division under Ms. Wood, who is the First Lieutenant. Traditionally, as long as the sea service has existed, the head of the deck department has been known as the First Lieutenant, regardless of his or her rank. And then myself, the Support Officer. When we get our ship structure to where we want it to be, which will require a couple more personnel, we'll have a Navigation Division and an Electronics Division as well within the Ops Department.

"Each of these departments is further broken down. For example, in the galley we have Chief Sorenson who is in charge. Beneath him are an FS1, or Food Service Specialist First Class, an FS2, and some FS3s. So if the FS3 needs something or has a problem, he or she is supposed to take it to the FS2, who takes it to FS1, to FSC, who brings it to me. Generally speaking, those problems are solved right at the level of their immediate supervisor. They only climb up the chain of command if that individual or the next one cannot solve it. So it is very efficient. It really does work. The meetings are generally pretty casual. For example, for this particular event, the Christmas Ship, there has been a planning meeting with the Captain, XO, and the Christmas Ship Committee, where they look at the overall big picture. More of the details of execution would come to me from, say, XO or the Operations Officer. The format and contents of meetings vary depending on what they are about. Each month we have a training board meeting where we schedule all of the training we are going to do for the coming month. We have the department heads and some other senior personnel there. It is pretty informal. It comes down to, 'All right EO, what kind of drills do you need? Ops what kind of drills do you need?' Some of them are a little bit more formal. That may come down to a chief's call, although there is an aura of mystery surrounding that ritual because only Chief Petty Officers are allowed in there. I think it is a little bit more organized than what we usually have. Typically the meetings are not too formal."

In your position as an administrator what are your main problems and opportunities?

"People, in both categories. The best part of the job, hands down, is working with great people. So often I will go to my Chief and say, 'Chief, we need to have this ready for tomorrow.' For example, for this event we need to have the wardroom ready for a breakfast and lunch with the Admiral present. Chief says, 'No problem,' and 'poof' magically it happens. It is executed beautifully. That is the best part of the job, working with quality people. The biggest problems/

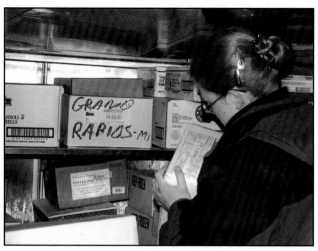

Here Molly performs her collateral duty and is doing an inventory of the ship's frozen foods.

challenges are also people. For every 99 really outstanding performers, which comprise the majority of the unit, we will have one or two problem children. It is generally very frustrating to deal with those people because there is a certain progression of steps that are supposed to be employed in working with them. For example Seaman Gooblatz (that is the stand-by name we like to use) doesn't get up in time for duty. You must counsel Seaman Gooblatz. The next time you issue Seaman Gooblatz a page that documents the episode to file in his record. It is a steady progression of documentation and counseling until Seaman Gooblatz is either sent to a Captain's Mast or, if Seaman Gooblatz really messes up, a Court Martial. Unfortunately, personnel issues such as that take up more of our time than any of us would like. It is said that 10% of our people take up 90% of our time, and it is absolutely the truth. Unfortunately, that 10% does not contain the great performers that you enjoy working with."

Let me ask you personally what process you went through to get here.

"I was a junior in high school at the time and I was starting to look at getting into college. My number one choice was the Colorado School of Mines. I was interested in becoming a metallurgist. I was shortly accepted to the School of Mines and had a scholarship there. Just to cover my bases I started applying to a lot of different schools. I had enlisted in the Army Reserve. I was going to use that to pay for college so I was going to the monthly drills, even throughout high school. I never had an open block throughout my high school career. I always completely filled my schedule with classes. I took the higher-level classes. I took the rigorous math and science program. I was actively involved with track and field, cross-country, drama, College Bowl, and music. I was receiving a good amount of correspondence from colleges

Deck watch officer Molly Killen

Molly, the captain and the XO

success or failure of a mission. My class was the last Coast Guard Academy class to send all of its graduates to sea. Since then, as the Coast Guard has been expanding, it has been forced to send graduates directly to flight school and to some shore billets. Given the option, I would have gone to sea all the same. I feel like this is the premier job in the Coast Guard. Maybe I am just biased, but I think this is the only way to go. I was looking at the majors available at the academy. There are some engineering majors there as well as electrical, mechanical, naval engineering. For me it came down to marine science and naval engineering. I ended up choosing marine science and studied chemistry and physical oceanography. But my focus shifted from the academic side of house at the academy to what I wanted to do with my career, as it typically does when you are progressing through. Pretty soon all you can think about is the fleet. I wanted to be a deck watch officer because that is how I will ascend to command. Engineers make the boat go. They know about every component of the ship. How it operates. If something goes wrong, they absolutely fix it. They are highly knowledgeable and highly skilled professionals. But I detest the thought of being stuck in the hole all day. I want to be in the sun and the wind. I want to be commanding movements of the ship. I want to learn classical seamanship. Eventually I want to become a commanding officer of larger and larger units."

How did the opportunity of the *Mackinaw* get in front of you?

"When the springtime of our first class year arrives we get what is called the shopping list. It is the list of available billets in the fleet that the newest graduating class will be able to go to. These billets are listed according to the unit, according to whether they can be filled by a man or woman, and according to whether they are deck or engineering. So I looked through the list and I chose *Mackinaw* because she struck me as a really multi-mission platform. She was in the north; I'm very much a cold weather person. I felt like I could learn a lot of different things on board. It really did parallel the way I made my decision to go to the Coast Guard Academy. Realistically speaking, I had very little information. She just kind of struck a chord with me. Again the decision turned out to be a good one because the 180-foot buoy tenders were previously considered to be the premier platform to learn how to be an outstanding ship handler. The last one has recently been retired. They have been replaced by ships that are navigated and piloted electronically. *Mackinaw*, on the other hand, requires some very serious ship handling skills. It was the northern climate, it was her capabilities, and I think because it was in a small town area away from a major metropolis that attracted me."

encouraging me to apply to their institutions. One day, among that daily pile of correspondence was a pamphlet from West Point. I previously had not considered any of the service academies. Just that fast, as soon as I saw that, it was like an epiphany. I decided, 'I am going to apply to West Point. In fact, I am going to go to West Point.' But again, in the spirit of covering all my bases, leaving no stone unturned, I applied to all the service academies, I applied to all of my congressmen for all of the appointments I could get. When all was said and done, I had three academy appointments and two congressional appointments. However, the Coast Guard was the only branch of the service that actually sent people to my home.

"An auxiliarist and an academy graduate arrived one evening at my home. They discussed the academy with my family and myself. They brought lots of great information, cleared up a lot of things. But the real clincher was a picture of the *Eagle*. At that point in time I was living in Colorado, I had grown up in the mid-west and western United States, very far away from a coast. I had never even seen a coast before. The biggest body of water I'd seen was a lake or farm pond. I had no idea that ships like that even existed. I had always been fascinated by piracy, by the lore of the sea. I saw *Eagle* and it was all over. I knew that would be the only opportunity I would ever get to sail on a ship like that. In fact, I made my decision with very little information. But at the same time, every day, I thank my lucky stars that I chose the way I did. I've always lived in small towns or outside of small towns. I've gone to small schools. And this small service with its small units is perfect for me. I have visited a couple of the other service academies. I visited some army bases, some air force bases. They are huge. They are absolutely gargantuan. I really feel as though I would just be a number in any other service. In the Coast Guard I am a larger portion of the operations and I matter more in the

The wardroom is officially the XO's space. The XO sits at the head of the table and the captain at his side. The officers eat their meals in this room. The XO relaxes here often with many of the guests aboard.

Is this your first duty and what would you tell a young person about life in the Coast Guard?

"It is. It is my first billet after graduating from the academy. I am 23 years old. I would say it does not matter where you go in the Coast Guard, where you are initially assigned. If you give it your all and maintain a positive attitude, and do the best work you possibly can, you will get to go wherever you want and do whatever you want in the Coast Guard. I would also say 'keep an open mind.' Sometimes you may be assigned a task or sent to a location that at first seems like a harbinger of doom when, in fact, it may be a job that is good for you or one that you will seriously enjoy. I have yet to encounter a duty that has turned out to be a very bad thing. Either it is fascinating or educational or it is good for one's professional development."

What was the most unexpected thing when you came to the *Mackinaw*?

"I would have to say it would be the wardroom environment. While we go through the academy we are groomed to be officers and gentlemen and officers and ladies. We have etiquette training. We are actually issued a thick etiquette book, called *Service Etiquette*. We are told, I will call it horror stories, about what it is going to be like in the wardroom out

in the fleet. This wardroom is absolutely not the uptight, stiff, nervous place I expected it to be. It is very relaxed. It is like a refuge. Everyone in there gets along very well. After I have had a tough and stressful morning I look forward to going to lunch. I sit down and enjoy a relaxing meal with people who are, in fact, my friends. We laugh, we tell jokes, we trade notes about the day. I can find out what is going on in engineering. The engineers can find out what is going on in the operations side of the house. It really is a very family-type atmosphere. We enjoy one another's company. The wardroom is a sanctuary to which we can return. That is, in fact, not the case in many cutters in the fleet. Lots of my classmates try to avoid the wardroom when they can, eat lunch in their stateroom or bring food on board and not get lunch from the galley at all. Sometimes the captain comes and sits down and says, 'Ensign entertain me.' That is not the case here. That is absolutely not the case here. It is more like, 'Captain, do you want to hear a joke?' And the captain will be glad to hear it. It was surprising in a very pleasant way."

What is the most memorable thing that has happened while you have been aboard?

"That one came right to mind. Last year the 1,000 foot taconite carrier *Edgar B. Speer* got stuck in the Rock Cut, part of the St. Mary's River. They figure she was grounded on ice, she was stuck so hard. We worked with her for about two days. A technique that we used to try to get her underway was to hitch ourselves to her bow with our towing hawser. Our goal was not to tow her out of there. Our goal was, instead, to hold ourselves in place so we could send a prolonged blast of prop wash against her bow so that we could wash some of that ice away. There we were, hitched to the bow of the *Edgar B. Speer*. We had gradually worked up the screws until we were at 130 turns. The tension gauge on our towing winch was reading about 70,000 pounds. We had 6 engines on-line. If we weren't at our 10,000-shaft horsepower limit, we were pretty close. We were making the world's largest Margarita, two massive whirling pools of slush at our stern. Large chunks of ice were coming up. It looked like we were gradually getting the job done. There were some very dirty chunks of ice too, indicating that we were washing big chunks of ice out from underneath. Then all of a sudden we heard this big 'boom'. Our hawser fell to the deck and we shot forward. Her towing pendant had broken. And that cable, that woven wire, was just splayed out at each end. Hers. We didn't break any of our gear; we broke three of the *Speer's* towing pendants that way though. It was an amazing testament to the power of this ship. How strong she really is."

Do you have any other adventure stories?

"Those beautiful sunny days where the sun is just glaring off all this ice that is the river and seeing this entire convoy of lakers behind you, following right in your path up the river. It is very satisfying. Going through the locks is always an adventure. You always feel a little bit nervous because the lock walls are so tight and close.

"At the end of the day, when we are done breaking ice, we like to run the engines really fast because that cleans all of the oil and junk out of them. It is like taking your car on a long interstate highway. It cleans the valves. A couple of times we have put the pedal to the metal toward the end of the day. I do recall bombing through about two feet of ice at about 12 knots. That was fun; that was a lot of fun. I've seen us cruise along at about 6 knots in three or four feet of ice up north of Drummond Island.

"Next year is going to be fascinating. I wish I could be around to watch the tandem trials with the new *Mackinaw*. A lot of people, myself included, don't have much faith in her just because she is so much smaller and has less gross tonnage. But what it comes down to is differences in technology and knowledge. When this mighty warrior was built, there was, maybe, one man who knew something about icebreaking and he was the professional consultant on the project. He said, 'You are going to need at least an inch of hull thickness on her.' They said, 'All right: 1-5/8ths.' It was a desperate time; they wanted to over-engineer her to make sure that she absolutely succeeded in her mission. Failure was not an option. Over the years, a lot more icebreakers have been built. Norway is building them. The Russians have built them. The United States has built them and we have collected a lot more data on how ice is actually broken, what the hull should be shaped like, how the propulsion plant works. So, although the new one is not as big and hefty as this one is, I don't think she necessarily needs to be. She is going to have a different type of propulsion. She is going to have a different shape of hull. She is going to be multi-mission capable. She will be able to work buoys. I think it is going to be fascinating to watch her work that first winter to see how she breaks the ice and how she does compared to

this cutter. I will be gone. This is going to be my last winter on board. I've enjoyed it.

"You know it has been a good watch when you come off the bridge with green hands. Our throttles are solid brass. So when you have your hands on those throttles the whole time, and you're sweating, and you are 100% tuned into the job at hand, your hands will turn green from that brass. That is the mark of a good watch right there."

The Mackinaw *has served as escort for the two annual yacht races.*

US Coast Guard

Artist among Scientist

by Molly Killen

Down in "the hole," the engineers' role is to study their tangle of pipes.
Valves and switches, machinery glitches – nothing's unknown to the snipes.
They have cheat sheets of numbers and manuals they lumber to watches and the frequent meetings.
Diagnostics and tests will ensure that they best all problems – recurring and fleeting.
The black and white, the wrong and right of "it works" or "damn thing's broken"
Leave no room to judge – engineers won't be budged once the techs and schematics have spoken.
Volumes of knowledge comprise the college on which the machinery techs are reliant.
Memorize and prevail, neglect and fail in this, the engineering science.

Rolling rules are the most primitive tools on which the navigator's rep is made.
"We're on track" or "off" and they'll never doff the proverbial lab coats of their trade.
A feeling or hunch they'll never begrudge, as they've no place on the plot.
The gaze berates as I often frustrate their efforts to put "X" on the spot.
To drive from the chart is the largest part of what the 'gators know as my skill
Graphs and tables, - not outdated fables – should comprise my manual of drill.
But at sea detail, the din doth pale as it's just me and Mack on the water.
Feel wind, current, turn – continue to learn the forces unknown to plotter.
The recommendation they make is fine for the lake – standard rudder, exactly twelve knots.
But I know how she moves, and my divergence soon proves with whom I've cast my lot.
While science is the foundation of safe navigation, the masters who've won my heart
Are teaching me the forces underlying the curses – to refine science by the addition of art.

John Wagner

White or red hull the Mackinaw's crew has performed her art and science.

The Mains

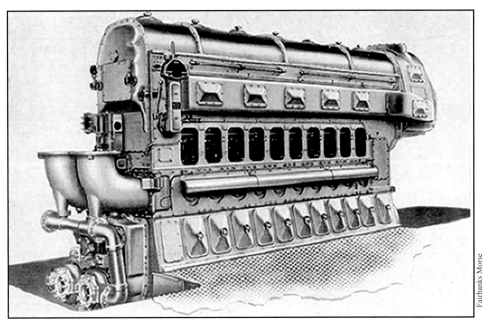

A Fairbanks Morse diesel engine of the type used on the Mackinaw. At 10 feet tall, 16 feet long, and only 30 inches wide, these engines are imposing. This is the inboard side of the engine from the control or exhaust end.

by Sandy Planisek

While the *Mackinaw* was temporarily docked at the tip of Navy Pier in Chicago I met two crewmen who are enthusiastically dedicated to their jobs. MK1 Lowery and MK2 Collins from #2 Space. It is important for me to identify the space number because there are three engine compartments on the boat and each has its own crew. They work their space and only reluctantly ascend to the second deck, cross the watertight bulkhead, and descend to work in another space. These spaces are not so creatively named: #1 Space, the most forward of the three, #2 Space and #3 Space.

Lowery and Collins were a working team. They were both incredibly helpful and offered to show me things or answer questions. They bubbled with so much pride they could do a Coast Guard TV ad. They asked for questions so I supplied them in a fast-moving stream of "why's," "how's," and "where's." Lowery presented me with his personal copy of "The Blue Jacket" and the little black *Mackinaw* fact book.

MK1 Lowery explains the engines to me.

The Mackinaw docked along the street in Chicago as Christmas Tree Ship.

actually standing near the ceiling of a deep well of a room with two huge, shiny, greenish-gray machines. The place is pretty well lit with sporadic florescent lights strung here and there. We went down a level, down another level and landed on the steel-plate runway that encircles the engines. Below us was the bilge and below that the lower tanks and hull. We were in a two-story room approximately 30 feet long and 50 feet wide. This single engine room is about 1600 square feet or the size of my house. But, unlike my house, this space is jammed with equipment: wires, pipes, motors, and gauges. They are all squeezed around the edges and are dominated by the all-powerful and all-consuming two engines. These huge gray monsters are 10 feet tall and 16 feet long. They nearly fill the room from fore to aft and take up the center third of the width. They dominate everything, including the three people that it takes to start them. These people circle the engines, like worker bees attending the queen bee, walking around and around on the safety-red steel-plate flooring attentive to the engines' every need.

A day later the *Mackinaw* was going to move up to the foot of Navy Pier, parallel to the street, for the actual ceremonies of Christmas Tree Ship. Lowery and Collins asked if I wanted to see "lite off." Again I had to ask for a definition. "Lite off" is the starting of the engines. They noted that an hour before the boat moves they will begin the 32-step checklist for starting the engines so at the appropriate time they would find me.

The door into the engine compartment is one level below the mess deck. As we stood at the door, Lowery reached over to a dispenser for earplugs. He explained that the engine rooms are loud; I would wear these rubber fingers in my ears, and then add a second level of protection with earmuffs.

The captain, they explained, was worried about the noise in the engine compartments, and had requested sound-level testing from headquarters. Unfortunately the testers arrived when the engines were quiet at the dock in Cheboygan. The captain sent them scooting and no testing had yet been completed.

Second, they warned me that the engine compartment was positively pressurized, something to do with exhaust, so the door would pop open into the passageway. This could be a problem when leaving the engine room since the door could pop open and hit an unsuspecting passerby. It was important to hold onto the door tightly. I learned later that once the engines are actually running they suck enough air to vacuum seal this same door occasionally making it difficult to open.

With that preparatory lesson the door was opened. Lowery went first, I followed, and Collins closed the door behind us. We were standing on a small platform made of steel mesh at the top of more stairs. A quick look showed me that I was

Air intakes

Captain McGuiness explaining the engines. These engines are tall and narrow, designed to fit comfortably on a railroad locomotive. At the top of the photo you can see the air intake on each of the engines. This photo is taken from the platform just inside the entry door near the top of the engine compartment.

While my eyes were filled with this wonder, my other senses were also sending urgent messages. The noise, even with the double ear protection, was deafening and we were restricted to screaming at each other and using hand signals. Of course the air was filled with the nauseating odor of diesel fuel. But most surprisingly the room was cold and the wind was blowing my hair into my eyes. Maybe that explains why these guys wear their hair so short.

Later, when we reemerged into the quieter world where communication was possible, they reminded me that diesel engines require a huge supply of air for combustion. These monsters are fed by large fans that blow exterior air into the space. The engines gulp air so quickly that the air in the engine room is the temperature of the outside air. This is the only place on the boat where I was ever cold. I was told that if it were snowing outside it also would be snowing inside.

Everything in the engine room is metal, of course, and you can see that these old engines are tired and allow some oil to escape. Yet after spending hours in #2 Space I didn't get any oil on my clothes or hands. The captain insists on cleanliness

Looking down at the engines toward the control end.

Here MK1 Cripe stands next to his engines in #3 Space. The near end is the control end of the engine, containing the starting lever and the exhaust ducts. The far end is called the blower end which is where the big generator is attached. The engine air intake and generator cooling air systems are attached on the blower end.

Seaman Collins standing at the desk area where check-off lists and temperature gauges are monitored at the control end of the engines.

Cut-away of one of the Mackinaw's engines

by Heinz Wernecke

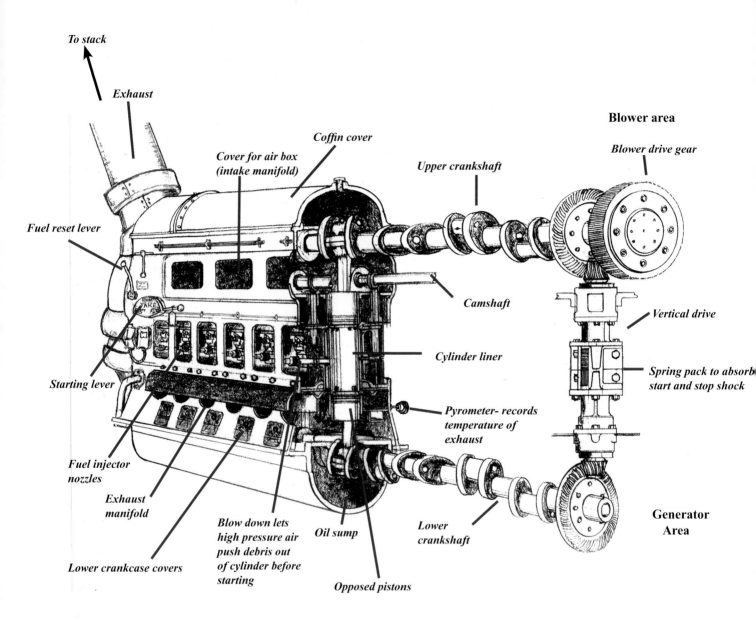

To stack

Exhaust

Blower area

Coffin cover

Blower drive gear

Cover for air box
(intake manifold)

Upper crankshaft

Fuel reset lever

Camshaft

Vertical drive

Cylinder liner

Spring pack to absorb
start and stop shock

Starting lever

Pyrometer- records
temperature of
exhaust

Fuel injector
nozzles

Exhaust
manifold

Blow down lets
high pressure air
push debris out
of cylinder before
starting

Oil sump

Lower
crankshaft

Generator
Area

Lower crankcase covers

Opposed pistons

and this crew was constantly wiping their space clean. The lighting in the space is uneven and guardrails are placed at turns and steps. The worn metal railings are so smooth, only years of hand rubbing could make pieces feels this soft, even silky. As I turned toward some of the gloomy corners of the room I could feel the presence of past crewmembers.

So how do these engines work?

These are the original 2-cycle Fairbanks Morse engines. They were built in the 1940s when diesel engines were just entering adulthood and the prime market was locomotives.

These engines are tall and narrow, only 30 inches wide. They are built to work long, hard, and steady on narrow railroad tracks. These two have been named Jake and Elwood by some long-forgotten crew. These engines are now 60 years old and, like all senior citizens, require more medical care. Parts can be replaced and have been, but these engines were purchased for World War II marine use and went into the *Mackinaw*, submarines and other specialty ships. Most of their co-classmates have already been retired so replacement parts are getting difficult to find. Casting new one-of-a-kind parts is very, very expensive. Yet the *Mackinaw*'s engines perform as well today as when new.

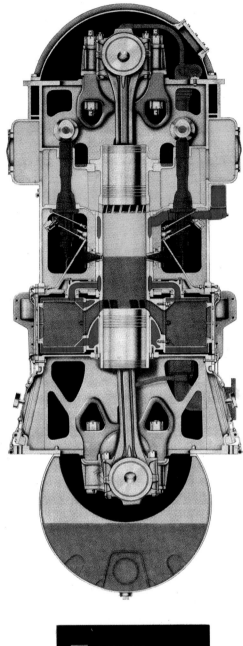

- LUBE OIL
- SCAVENGING AIR
- FRESH WATER
- FUEL OIL
- EXHAUST GAS

Fairbanks Morse

A quick look at how the engine works. It is cooled with water, called jacket water, and oil. It is officially called a Fairbanks Morse 38D 8 1/8. The bore on this engine is 8-1/8 inches and the stroke is 10 inches.

They are not refined machines, which might explain why the crew is so dedicated to them. They are simple, straightforward, and massive. Taking them apart is heavy work that requires knowledge of engines and block & tackle (called chain falls since the tackle is made up of chain, not rope) but all parts are big enough to see, hold, and replace. No miniaturization, no fancy electronics. The crew does every bit of maintenance. Their engines are their work. No wonder each engine compartment has its loyal following.

The future *Mackinaw* will be different. Factory experts will maintain engines. This will be more efficient with less chance of error and undoubtedly will breed far less loyalty. No 60-year reunion of 400 former crewmembers for a boat whose broken parts are pulled out and sent in to distant experts. Where is the honor and pride in that?

The *Mackinaw* has six engines. A routine summer run down the lake will involve two engines with two on standby. Four engines are always running when the *Mackinaw* enters a river or narrow channel. All six engines are used for tricky maneuvering and for extra power during ice breaking. A rotation assures that all engines are treated equally and get their fair share of work hours.

The crew will quickly tell you that these engines are 10-cylinder, in-line opposed piston engines. These engines do NOT drive the propellers. They drive generators that make DC electricity that is used to run electric motors that drive the propellers.

It sure sounded convoluted to me until I found and read the training manual.

First, why don't the engines drive the propellers? Car engines drive the wheels, albeit with a transmission between. Ferryboat engines drive the propellers, again with transmissions. Why doesn't that work for the *Mackinaw*?

Originally, according to the training manual, diesel engines did drive the propellers in Naval vessels. "This design, known as direct drive, developed immediate operational problems. The hull characteristics definitely fixed the angle of the propeller shafting. This restriction also determined engine position and location. Also, the most efficient propeller speeds did not correspond with the most efficient engine speeds."

Therefore engineers went to work on two problems
1. How to separate the propeller shaft from the engine
2. How to allow different rotational speeds for the propeller and the engine.

The Navy tried many things but found that the diesel-electric drive worked best. Not only did it solve the above problems but also it separated the propellers from the engine vibration and allowed the propellers to be reversed without having to stop and reverse the engines, a difficult and dangerous operation.

So the boat has both engines and motors. The three motors, located out in the ends of the boat, are dedicated to, and bolted to, their propellers. The diesel engines, located in the center of the boat, produce electricity that can be routed to the three electric propulsion motors. This provides welcome redundancy and flexibility. This configuration allowed the designers to place all of the engines low down in the center of the boat for best stability.

Now, what about those 10-cylinder opposed pistons? The *Mackinaw's* engines have one crankshaft on the top connected to the top 10 pistons and a second crankshaft on the bottom connected to the bottom 10 pistons. Several crewmembers illustrated this by pushing their two fists together, opposite each other. The pistons are timed to approach each other simultaneously, compressing the air-fuel mixture until it explodes creating the driving power of the engine.

Why opposed? Again the training manual explains it well, " . . . the opposed piston engine has three distinct advantages:

1. It has higher thermal efficiency than engines of comparable ratings (i.e. more power from each gallon of fuel)

2. It eliminated the necessity of cylinder heads and intricate valve mechanisms with their cooling and lubricating problems

3. There are fewer moving parts."

But opposed pistons mean two crankshafts. How does that work? The crankshafts are hooked together by a vertical drive mechanism that keeps the crankshafts in time with

Lowery has the red tag on Jake while it is being repaired.

each other; however, each crankshaft has a slightly different set of duties. The extra mechanisms of the engines, such as cams to manage the fuel pumps, air intake blowers, etc are driven off of the top crankshaft. Thus 70% of the propulsion power comes off the lower crank which leads the upper by 12 degrees.

The engines performed nicely during the Chicago cruise but icebreaking is tough work. Ram, ram, back, and ram. The engines take a beating. Always concerned by this heavy wear, the crew routinely practices safety drills. They were performing a drill that simulated an injured crewmember in the engine room. In the process of the drill Jake, engine #3, backfired and a crewmember really was hit by flying debris. The drill turned into actuality. The need for drills was reinforced. The backfire also meant that Jake would need a "ring job" as soon as the ship was back at home port.

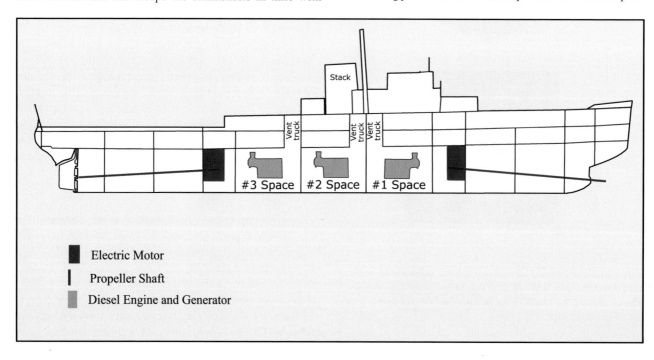

Jake was torn apart during mid-winter repair season in late February.

I was lucky enough to be able to watch and photograph this process. No engines were running so the noise level was quite pleasant. The air temperature was also pleasant. The work crew varied from three people to 10 people.

The dismantling process started with removing the top, called the coffin cover. The top set of pistons was unbolted from the crankshaft and the crank was lifted off, all 2,500 pounds of it. The top pistons were pulled up and out while the bottom pistons were snaked out of lower covers.

In taking off the old rings the crew discovered that some of the rings had been installed upside down! This explained why the deck crews always complained when Jake was fired up. The excess oil that was spewed out of the stack and onto the deck was not caused by engine wear but by incorrect ring placement. The correctly placed rings should solve the excessive oil problem.

These kinds of errors happen. Crewmembers only spend three years working on the *Mackinaw* and never really conquer the intricacies of the job. This is the argument for using outside contractors or manufacturer representatives to maintain the equipment.

The total engine job took approximately two weeks. It was steady work. Lifting 100-pound pistons and torquing huge nuts was a physical workout. Yet precision also was required. Tolerances on the crankshaft, for example, are only 3/1000 of an inch. Everything had to be perfectly clean, measured and remeasured for exact tolerances. Anything found that was out of acceptable range had to be repaired or replaced. The cost of a mistake is high. One crankshaft alone is valued at $100,000.

The work pace accelerated towards the end of the repair because one of the smaller icebreakers needed repairs and, as always, the *Mackinaw* stepped in.

Before the ring job a 30-hour trip to Chicago deposited this much oil on the walls on the back deck of the boat. It no longer does this.

There is just enough head room in the engine compartment to walk across the top of the engine once the crankshaft is removed. Notice a piston sitting to this crewmember's left.

*Jake, the engine on the right in #2 Space, was rebuilt in 2005. The two forground workers remove the rings from the pistons.
Central is one of the pistons with its connecting rod sticking up. The back two workers are pulling out the lower pistons. The
drill-like tool in the foreground is called a barring tool. It uses high pressure air to rotate the engine for easier access to parts.
The upper crank shaft, which has been removed, is in the middle of this photo. This photo is taken from the blower end near the
generators.*

Lowery is standing on top of the engine and explaining the timing chain.

The pieces of the engine must be kept orderly. The 10 cylinder parts are not necessarily interchangeable so all are numbered and kept in order. These are the bearings from where the connecting rods attach to the crankshaft.

I am shooting a photo of the bearings on the end of the piston arms with the help of CWO Woodworth while standing on the entry level deck. Below me, three crewmen are working on the lower pistons. These engines are huge. The orange block and chains are positioned in order to lift the crankshaft.

Lite Off

by Sandy Planisek

My first lite off left me with the following information:

This process involves turning a dozen or so wonderful, large, brightly colored wheels in the proper order apparently to open and close valves.

Blow down is a step before starting that sends a smoky cloud into the room.

The exciting moment is when the big brass throttles are moved first to start and then to run.

That is not to be confused with the moment of "excitation" which I still don't quite understand. Something about the magnetism of the generators. . .

While my understanding of this process is a bit weak, I did learn that a check-list is followed each and every time the engines are started. In my journey of learning and living with the *Mackinaw* I met an email friend, Bob Hughes, who served on the *Mackinaw* in the 1950s. He sent me a description process from his memory.

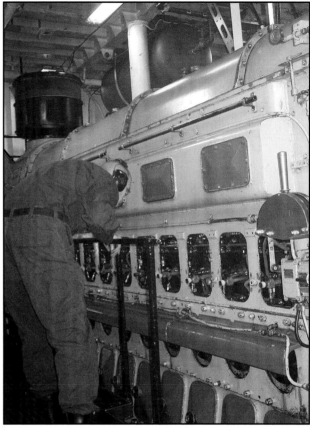

Before starting the engines high pressure air is sent into the piston liners to blow out any dirt or oil that might have settled in. Called blow-down, this process puts a haze into the air. Here MK2 Collins is preparing for lite off.

Valve turning is part of the starting process.

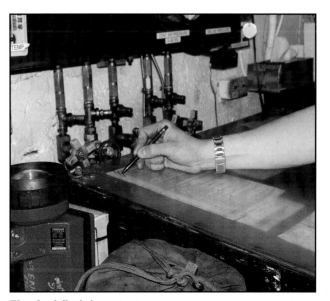

The check list is important.

Sandy,

I was surprised to hear that you witnessed the lite off procedure while in Chicago. It has been about 45 years since I was last working on the *Mackinaw*, but I will try to describe the procedure as best as I can. At that time the *Mackinaw's* main engines were Fairbanks-Morse Model 38D8&1/8 diesel engines. I have no way of knowing if they still use the same engines.

Usually a few hours prior to lite off, the lube oil heaters and engine jacket water heaters would be activated to warm up these systems prior to lite off. I believe both systems were heated by steam from the boilers in engine room #2.

1. When it was time for lite off, all necessary sea chest valves for seawater intake, overboard discharge, etc. would be opened.

2. The lube oil circulating pumps would be turned on until oil pressure was indicated on the control panel to pre-lubricate the engine bearings prior to lite off.

3. With the individual cylinder blow-down valves open, the engine would be cranked over to discharge any excess fuel or water leakage from the cylinders. The fuel injector racks would be disengaged during the blow-down. After blow-down, the valves would be closed and the injector racks reengaged.

4. When a start bell from the bridge or other signal to lite off was received, the throttle man would move the throttle handle from the stop to start position activating the high pressure air distributors to crank the engine over until it started, then the handle would be moved to the run position. During this operation, he would hold the low oil pressure alarm lever down to the off position to keep the alarm siren from sounding until proper pressure was obtained.

5. After the engines were running, their generators were connected to the respective main motors. My memory here is a little vague, but I believe this was done on the control panel in the motor room. The engines in engine room #1 could be connected to the bow propeller shaft from the forward motor room or they could be connected to the stern propeller shafts from the after motor room. Engine rooms #2 and #3 could only be connected to the stern shafts.

6. Since high pressure starting air was used to start the engines, sometimes if the bridge signaled for all six engines at the same time, the high-pressure air would be depleted before all engines started. A savvy throttle man would have his assistant hold the fuel racks for a couple of cylinders partially open to give an added boost for starting.

Bob Hughes

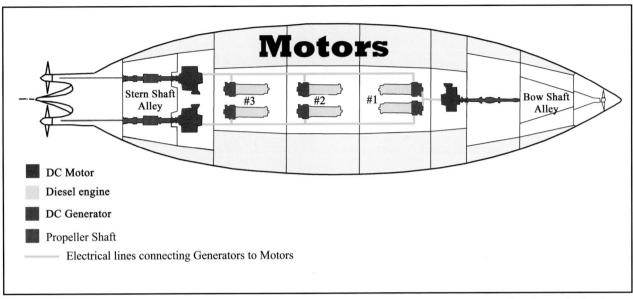

Motors

Stern Shaft Alley

#3   #2   #1

Bow Shaft Alley

■ DC Motor

▨ Diesel engine

■ DC Generator

■ Propeller Shaft

――― Electrical lines connecting Generators to Motors

The engines are located low and central in the Mackinaw. The electrical motors, on the other hand, are directly attached to the propellers. Any and all of the three engines on the port side of the boat can send their electrical output to the aft port motor and hence propeller. Likewise, the three starboard-side engines can power the starboard aft propeller. The two forward engines, which sit backwards in their space, can also power the forward propeller.

by Sandy Planisek

The huge Fairbanks Morse engines on the *Mackinaw* are the main players in the icebreaking drama. They demand attention by their sheer size, their temperament, and their pretensions. They claim to be the main power source for the *Mackinaw*. They even carry the nickname "mains."

But this is a misleading claim. They are indeed critical to the movement of the ship, but they are not the power that makes the ship move. Their role is like the interpreter in a major international event; they are facilitators. They translate the energy taken aboard as low-cost diesel fuel into a more portable and controllable energy, electric power. Even in this task they cannot achieve the goal alone. They are bolted to huge generators that actually produce the electricity. There is no clutch; there is no transmission, the rotational speed of the engine is the rotational speed of the generator.

Each generator creates 900 volts and 1530 amps of direct current, DC, electricity. In our everyday lives we encounter direct current in the batteries we use, the 9-volts in our smoke detectors or 12-volts in our car batteries. These appear weak compared to the 900-volt system used on the *Mackinaw*. If these generators weren't busy powering a ship they could power about 2,000 homes, a town twice as big as Mackinaw City. Of course, homes usually don't use DC power.

The blue-gray generator is geared directly to the greenish engine. They are partners in producing electrical power which flows off through the white cables.

If the engine-generator combination simply produces DC electricity, what actually powers the ship? Here enters the unsung hero of our story, the three Westinghouse propulsion motors, one on each propeller shaft. There are two of these electric motors in the stern, each with the potential to produce 5,000 horsepower and turn the propellers up to 136 revolutions per minute. A third, smaller bow motor is capable of producing 3,300 horsepower and spins the bow prop up to 175 rpms. Propeller speeds are similar to the speeds of a ceiling fan, but these underwater fans easily push the *Mackinaw* through ten feet of ice. While the *Mackinaw* will never set a speed record, all of this horsepower is applied at this slow speed which means POWER!

Engineering Department

by Don Witt, Senior Chief Electrician

"I'm in the engineering department so I stand engineering watches. I'm also the head of the electrician shop. Because the *Mackinaw* is diesel-electric the main engines drive the propulsion generators that produce direct current, DC, electricity. The electricity is carried by cable to the propulsion motors that turn the shafts. I'm in charge of the electrical side, the generators and motors. I am also in charge of the ship's service power, the alternating current, AC, that powers the lights, motors, and fans. The distribution system for that includes switchboards, circuit breakers, the power panels, and the fuse panels. I also maintain the gyrocompass and some of the interior communications such as sound-powered phone circuits."

What is the advantage of diesel-electric and particularly DC? Why is this boat designed that way?

"Diesel-electric has advantages over regular, what we call "reg gear" type. If you don't have diesel-electric you need a mechanical link all the way from your engines to your shaft. That means your engines have to be down low and back, fairly close to where your shaft goes through the hull. With diesel-electric you can position your engines anywhere. You can have three engine rooms, like we have, because all you do is run cabling between the generators and the motors. With our configuration we have six main engines. We can have one, two, or three engines on each aft shaft. Or we can take our two forward engines and put them both on our bow shaft. There is more flexibility."

Why DC over AC?

"*Mackinaw* was designed 60 years ago when they didn't have the technology for AC. A DC motor is fairly simple, the

The engines are the heart of this machine but the motors are the muscle. The 12-foot tall Westinghouse propulsion motors occupy two rooms and are air cooled with massive intake fans.

Compare this drawing of the stern propulsion motor (with the cooling cover off) with the photo above to see just how large this motor is. Notice the two holes near the top in both photos to equate the scale.

more voltage you put to it the faster it will go. To increase the speed of an AC motor you have to increase the frequency of the electrical current. That technology has only been around maybe 20 or 30 years.

"With DC electric there is a lot of maintenance. That is the reason they are going to AC electric. When you deal with DC electric you are using brushes to pass current to the rotating armature. While it is rotating it is wearing down those brushes, putting dust into the air. The carbon dust is conductive so, if it lands on a surface, it will eventually ground out your system. You won't go until you clean it. We have a maintenance period every three months when we will take all the covers off the main motors and the main generators and clean them. If you have electrical grounds in your propulsion system you are dead in the water."

The bow propeller shaft continues forward and exits the hull here. Because of its extreme length it has to have small bearings, pillow blocks like shown here, to keep it from bending under its own weight.

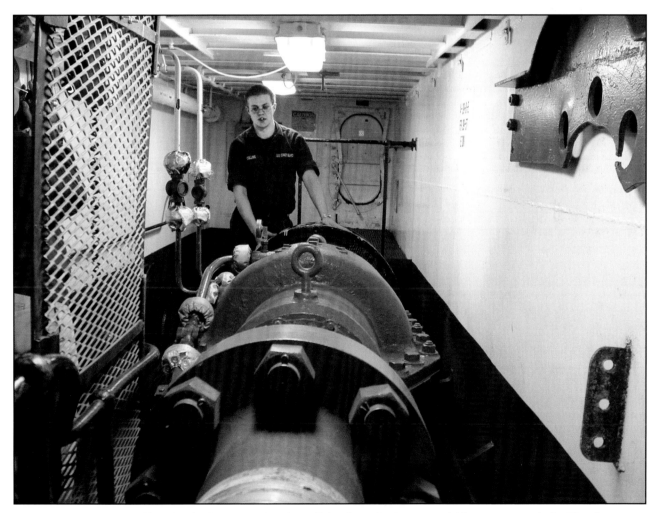

The bow propeller shaft is 13 inches in diameter and perhaps 40 feet long. In the center of this compartment is the Kingsbury thrust bearing which takes the forward power created by the propeller and transfers it to the hull. Thus, both the propeller shaft and the ship move forward through the water. Hanging on the wall in the upper right is a propeller shaft lock. It keeps the propeller from moving while repairs are underway. It fits over the bolts in the foreground and prohibits their spinning by locking to the wall at right. It obviously has been used and abused in the past. This photo is taken looking forward.

The Rudder

by Sandy Planisek

With forward momentum provided by the propellers, the problem now becomes steering this voluptuous 5,252-ton ice crusher. Any boat handler will tell you that twin-props make steering easy. Combinations of forward and reverse on the two stern motors will allow the ship to turn in almost any configuration. Indeed, the use of the stern props guides the *Mackinaw* gently up to the dock in Cheboygan. Where maneuverability is even more constrained, the bow prop and starboard aft prop can produce a snappy sideways glide to the dock.

Although the conning officer's art for sideways movement is a point of pride, it is only worth the trouble when approaching the dock. In open water, steering is done with the rudder. The *Mackinaw's* single rudder is a mammoth 12 feet 2 inches tall and 9 feet 6 inches wide. It is wedge shaped with the leading edge a substantial 18 inches narrowing to a delicate 4-inch wide trailing edge. The rudder is balanced on the rudder post which itself is over one foot in diameter.

The helmsman on the bridge spins the ship's wheel and a hydraulic piston eases the rudder in response.

by MK1 Backlas

"When the boat was in dry dock they dropped the rudder out. We cut a hole in the main deck and built an A-frame. There is a threaded hole in the top of the rudderpost where you can put a lifting eye. We hooked it all up and then unbolted the tiller arms and we slowly lowered the rudder out of the bottom of the boat down onto the ground."

The rudder post drops right down out of after-steering

As the crew paints the depth numbers on the side of the hull they give scale to the thickness of the rudder which is just protruding above the water line.

A spare set of the all-steel props and shafts is stored in Baltimore. They appear to be rather rusty. It is expected that they will be gviven to the museum ship.

The rudder on the Mackinaw sits on the centerline of the boat and is about 12 feet tall and about 9 feet wide. The keel protects it from ice while the boat is moving forward.

tiller arm   rudder post   cooling fan

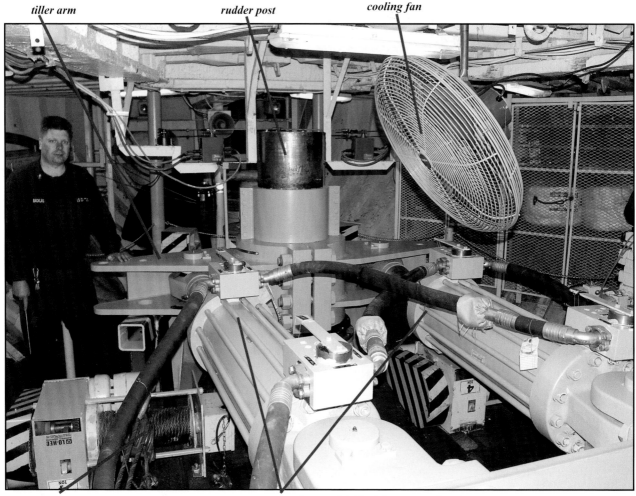

electric winch   two pistons with black hoses carrying the oil

This is the after-steering compartment, the last place on the boat. The boat's notch protrudes into this room The solid steel rudder post pierces the water tank below this room and then on through the hull. The room is protected from flooding by water-tight seals. A tiller connects to the rudder post with keyways. A redundant system of two hydraulic pistons push and pull on the tiller. In case the hyraulics fail, an electric winch can center the rudder where it can be locked amidships. The rudder can swing 32 degrees in 21 seconds. The propellers are under this floor at about the location of the photographer. This aft compartment is single-hulled and during ice breaking the noise level is as high as in the engine rooms.

The old steering mechanism was a large gear, called a quadrant, encircling the rudder post. This gear was badly worn so steering was sloppy. It was changed in 2000. In the right foreground is the DC drive motor for the gear.

Main Control

by Sandy Planisek

As I finally had some understanding of the decision making role the bridge makes in operating the ship, I began to couple that knowledge with the information on how the engines and motors operate. But that left one piece of the puzzle unexplained: the motor rooms.

One clue to their importance was that everyone wanted to make sure I had seen them. And that was no easy feat. There are three of them and they are each located alongside one of the huge propulsion motors. They are low in the boat,

below the level of decent staircases and into the world of the vertical ladder. They are at the far ends of the boat, where the motors are attached to the propellers.

My first visit was during lite off in Chicago. We were running all six engines and all three shafts so everyone was busy. LTJG Lawrence offered to take me to see "Main Control." Main Control is the main switchboard in the starboard motor room. The other motor rooms also have

Green indicates the engines are on-line, in this case all six.

Switchboard wall

Security camera looking at mast

CWO Woodworth, EMCS Witt, and MKMC Hamerle in Main Control..

Buzzers to alert people in noisy spaces

switchboards but they don't perform all of the functions of Main Control. We arrived at Main Control to find a tiny room about the size of a king-sized bed. One wall was the switchboard and crammed in front of it were three people. The space was so small that one person was seated on a chair mounted up high above another piece of equipment, allowing more floor space for the others.

The main wall switchboard was covered from floor to ceiling with dials, lights, gauges, and steering wheels the size of a go-cart's. At 90 degrees to this was another wall partially covered with lights and below it, on the floor, was a long torpedo shaped object. Lastly, hanging in another corner near the ceiling was a TV monitor. When I arrived all eyes were on the TV monitor. They explained that we were looking at the mast through the eyes of the boat's security monitors. What we were seeing was one of the young officers high up on the mast trying to drag a Christmas tree up to tie to the mast for the upcoming festivities. We could hear the young officer who was struggling to pull up the tree while clinging to the swaying mast. He certainly didn't want to find out if his safety harness would really work in a fall. Ultimately, another person went up to help. The tree was finally put in place and we were ready.

Then voices entered the room, apparently people from the bridge talking, but they were so hard to hear and understand. The Master Chief, sitting in the chair, had earphones and was apparently able to hear because he was talking back. After a little back and forth conversation red lights began to turn green, the steering wheels were turned and we started to move.

This room and these people were obviously a critical link in the process of making the boat move but I did not really understand their role until I sat down to write this book. This space acts as a duplicate, albeit below water, bridge. From here the engines can be controlled and the steering control can be sent to the rudder room. Second, this room "balances the plant" meaning they make sure that all of the engines are doing their fair share of the work. This is the only place on the boat where all of that balancing work can be done.

Dials indicating amps, and air for each of the three starboard engines

RPMs for all three propellers

Chadburn connected to the one on the bridge

Speed control transfer lever lets the engineer determine whether the bridge or the motor room controls the speed of the boat

Maple wood safety grab bars

The motor room switchboard. The three big wheels actually turn mechanical plates with relay switches. As the wheels turn, the switches make contact with different wiring options.

by MK1 Backlas

"A modern system is probably all computer-controlled but this is 1940s technology and the computers were all up here (pointing to his head). Back then the computers didn't come from Japan we grew our own, our people."

MK1 Backlas shows the back side of one of the switchboards. These are the original White Westinghouse and General Electric switches. At the far end is the vertical tubing which holds the air used to power the governors on the engines. It is amazing to realize that this 60-year-old wiring is still in working order.

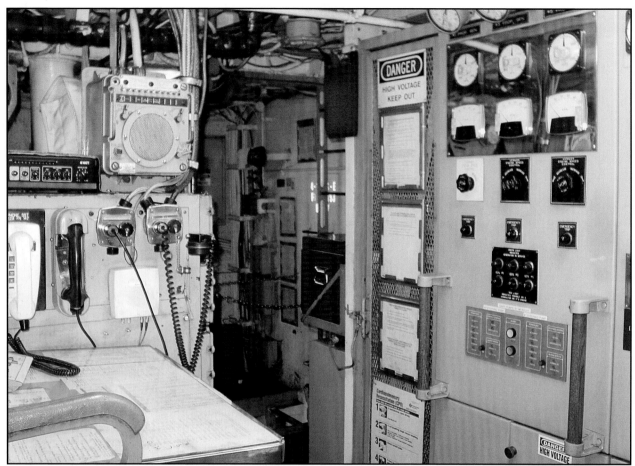

The switchboard view from the chair shows that this person has access to several communication devices including regular telephones, VHF radios, sound-powered phones, and the squawk box.

MK1 Backlas points to the exciter which activates the magnetic field in the generators and motors before starting. This is also squeezed into Main Control.

The sound-powered phone system is an antique which is ready for use at all times. The signal is powered by the talker's voice.

Engineering Officer
LCDR Mike Barner

by Mike Barner

"I am LCDR Mike Barner. I'm the engineering officer for the Cutter *Mackinaw*. I have been on the cutter for two years. I am responsible for the engineering department and I am responsible for the engineering plant. It is a general title that is all encompassing."

How did you end up being here?

"I grew up in a military family. My father was a marine and my brother recently retired from the Air Force. I applied to all of the academies' scholarship programs in high school. I chose the Coast Guard Academy because the Coast Guard is always performing humanitarian missions. I like the role of the Coast Guard over the other DOD (Department

The crew, including Mike Barner, cut the Christmas trees delivered to Chicago during Christmas Tree Ship.

of Defense) services. When I originally graduated in 1994 I requested *Mackinaw*. Then they announced that the ship was being decommissioned and the assignments were pulled off the list. So I got my second chance to apply again two years ago. It has always been a goal for me to serve on the *Mackinaw*. Since then I learned more about the ship and I was really excited that it is a one-of-a-kind antique icebreaker. I was surprised when I got the assignment."

What were your expectations?

"Most of my assignments have been very technical, where I apply personal technical expertise. This job has been more leadership, personnel management. I supervise 43 people and it is my job to make sure they get taken care of, they get paid, their families are taken care of with housing, and that they have the training and tools to do their job. I have to get them the funding for the projects we need to accomplish for the ship. I am not a wrench turner on the ship. I actually set the pace for the department. I see 70% of my job as people, 20% of it is working to get us funding, to plan our long-term maintenance and improvement projects, while only about 10% of it is hands-on technical direction. The crew does such a good job that there is very little actual hands-on involvement. The petty officers and chiefs are specific area experts."

Have the problems been what you expected?

"Yes, the problems have been what I anticipated. I anticipated age-related problems and that is exactly what we had. The last few engineers have worked really hard to identify the projects. When I first got here I followed through on the planned projects of the engineer before me. Then I identified my own set of priorities and set about working on them. The ship was in disrepair after the mid-80s to mid-90s. The Coast Guard had applied to decommission the ship several times. It wasn't getting the proper funding and maintenance. Ever since, we have been bringing the ship back up to where it should be. It culminated this ice season. We had the entire plant working long and hard the entire ice season without any problems. Now the ship is 100% operational just in time for decommissioning. (Smile)

"My biggest learning curve was learning to work with the enlisted members and helping them with their problems. It is my job to identify the successes and reward the really good work. It is also my job to identify disciplinary problems. We have about 10% that have discipline problems. These are people that are 18 to 25 years old and are still developing. It is our role to apply discipline to either help them develop or move them on to their next career."

What about the good people?

"The expertise on this ship is just amazing. I really have a lot of respect for everybody who has worked on the ship. They are going off to fill really

Taking the time to come to the bridge and see the world as the captain does.

important jobs after the ship. Ninety percent of the people leaving this ship are going to their 1st, or 2nd, or 3rd choice assignment. That says we have quality people who competed really well for really good jobs."

How does the Coast Guard train you for these positions?

"There are some training opportunities that you should go to before you go to an assignment. That mostly prepares you for the paperwork. The paperwork is the easy side. The leadership side you learn on the fly, through experience. I really had a lot of help from CDR McGuiness when I first got here. He really helped me. I was straightforward when I got here and told him I didn't have a lot of experience supervising petty officers. He walked me through the first couple of months until I could handle what I was doing."

What is the most rewarding part of your job and the biggest problem?

"When people succeed. When the crew makes the ship run. We just got back from several weeks of icebreaking and really every one of us were waiting for the problem to develop, something to go wrong with the plant. It just didn't happen. That was really a rewarding ending to all of the years of work and making maintenance improvements, the long hours, the weekends, and the summer deployments training the crew. Everybody knew his or her job. All the equipment worked. We didn't have any causalities (equipment failures) which is really remarkable. We are used to dealing with causalities. We joke and call this 'Coast Guard Cutter MacGyver' because we have to figure out creative fixes to problems other ships just simply don't have.

The inside view can be beautiful.

"The biggest problems we had last year were with the main engines. We had problems with the piping, the raw water system, jacket water piping. The piping was just old and deteriorated. You put the engines under a lot of strain and either the pressure or temperature causes a rupture. We would have ruptures where we would have to secure the engines and repair it. Last summer we went through all those systems and identified all of the problems where people before us had MacGuyvered it and gotten whatever fittings were available on hand to fix the problem in their face. We went back and removed whole sections of fitting to fitting to fitting to fitting and put in continuous pipe.

"The remarkable things about the ship are the amazing back-up systems, tertiary systems, and the safeties to make sure we don't overload the engines or generators. The whole propulsion system is essentially original. The propulsion switchboards are all original, the original wire, even the original tags in there. It is remarkable to look at. The systems that had to be replaced are mostly piping systems. They have a life expectancy. Things that have water in them will rust. We also have problems balancing the ship service generators, the ones that make the AC power used by the lights and things. The original generators were replaced in the 70s or 80s and when the new system was installed, a computer-balancing program was installed. At the time it was a good system. Now that system is grossly outmoded. We have weekly problems with this system, the 'Modicon system'.

"One remarkable system is the shaft cooling system. We actually pump raw water to the shafts for cooling and flushing of the shafts. The primary system is a pump that sucks from the #3 engine room sea chest for the aft shafts and the #1 engine room sea chest, for the bow shaft. If there is a problem with the sea chest we can actually lite off a fire pump in another engine room and draw off that sea chest and cross connect it to the shaft core. If there is a problem with

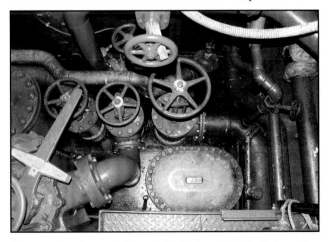

The sea chest is a port through the bottom of the hull through which lake water is brought into the boat. Sea chests tend to freeze up during ice breaking. They are also the ports through which the warm water, after cooling the engines, is discharged. Thus, this area is a maze of piping.

The wire chase through the mess deck is a huge bundle of wires from all of the decades of the boat's life. The red pipe is a water line for fire suppression.

all the sea chests, we can draw from the heel tanks by realigning the piping. It is a tertiary system. It is really interesting that they thought of that.

"The ship is 60 years old and has much of the original electrical wiring in the ship. My largest concern is the electrical wiring. We have regular problems with the fuses and some with the wiring. We have done a lot with removal of old deadend cables. But there are still a lot. It isn't a problem, but it is a concern. You can look at most of the cable runs and tell the history of the ship. You can see some of the original armored cable painted white. You can see other generations of cable added to it, all the way up to brand new computer cable run a few years ago."

Do you have special memories?

"The highlights were definitely the icebreaking seasons. The biggest thrill for everyone on the crew, myself included, is getting out and walking around the ship when we are hove-to in the ice. That is pretty remarkable to stand in front of the ship and look at the ship from the ice perspective. That is a highlight for everybody.

"My own personal highlights are successes with people. I am really pleased that they all got good next assignments. It is always exciting when a crewmember has a child or a major event in their family. We become a

Look in and see the old copper air tubes that still make the throttles work.

family and I have enjoyed that part of it. There are at least five that I know I will be working with in the next year or two. The Coast Guard is small and we end up seeing each other again and again. We are definitely a name and face here as opposed to the other services where you are just a number."

What would you tell a touring visitor?

"The 60 years of hard work is important. Everyone takes a tour to the bridge and looks out from the bridge. People should definitely look into the ship as well to see what actually makes this ship run. Look at the different spaces on the ship and uses of the ship. Consider how the ship was originally designed and how we modified it. It was originally designed for a crew of 120 men and now we are a crew of 75 men and women. There are a lot of alterations that have happened during that time. It was definitely less comfortable than it is today."

Pumps and pipes have needed attention.

A-Gang

by Mike Backlas

"I am MK1 Backlas, Machinery Technician First Class. I'm the auxiliary shop supervisor. The auxiliary shop takes care of all hotel services on the boat: potable water, refrigeration, air conditioning. We also take care of all the hydraulic systems on *Mackinaw,* including the steering system. We take care of the boat davits, high AB crane, hydraulic winches, the big towing winch, all the galley equipment, all the lube oil systems, and the fuel oil system. Our nickname is A-gang. We take care of the behind the scenes stuff that makes the whole thing work. Fortunately, I have a lot of great skilled people working for me in the shop. There are five us of in A-gang. We maintain the engines and drive systems for the ship's small boats, the Mack 1, the Mack 2 and the ice skiff.

"The A-gang is responsible for all of the oily waste on the boat. We have a waste water system oil-water separator. We maintain that. We get rid of all the excess water we pick up. We are responsible for all of the hazardous materials on the *Mackinaw.*

"Take the refrigeration on the boat. We converted the old system over to 134a to eliminate the older environmentally unfriendly coolant. We have scroll compressors and updated controls, but it is a modified old system. And it works! We

MK1 Backlas spent five hours with me explaining throttles, the towing winch, and how the A-gang works. A-gang is that section of the engineeering department responsible for all equipment except the engines and electrical service. They handle all piping, pumps, air handling, hydraulics, welding, fabrication, and on and on. They probably have the widest diversity of tasks on the boat.

"This is the auxiliary machine shop. This is where the A-gang will restore our tools, where we do our office work. This is where we keep the spare parts, gaskets, all the things we need to go around the ship and maintain the systems."

got it working. It works great. The ice cream doesn't melt. (Smile)

"But it is like anything else. A new house is a new house. An old house that has been remodeled is still an old house that has been remodeled. But, the old house that has been remodeled probably has more charm. And that is what I think *Mackinaw* has, charm."

The King of Fuel and Water

by Sandy Planisek

The Christmas Tree Ship stop in Chicago marks the end of the public affairs season and the beginning of the icebreaking season for the *Mackinaw*. Using their shore leave while in Chicago, the coasties spread out according to their tastes. Some took the bait of free museum admissions to visit the Field Museum, the Aquarium and smaller specialty museums. Some shopped on Navy Pier and nearby Michigan Ave. and a few took the opportunity to relax on the boat.

With fewer people on the ship, a peace settled in. Personal space increased to a more comfortable level. Crewmembers were sitting alone rather than clumped in groups. It was easer for me to approach individuals for an interview. I roamed the boat as casually as possible, given my burden of a video camera mounted on trip-hazard tripod legs. I poked into an exceptionally large office, the engineering office, and saw a fellow studying a computer screen.

"Can I interrupt you?" "Sure." Everyone was willing to take time to talk to me. Perhaps they had discretionary time since we were sitting in Chicago, but I would like to think that pride in their work pushed open a hole in their schedule so the ship's story could be recorded.

MK3 Pietrolungo works on manpower deployment.

"I am MK3 Pietrolungo and I am in charge of the fuel and water systems. I am the king."

"The king?" "Yes, the fueling king," he said with a twinkle in his eyes. Pietrolungo is a short, quiet guy who smiles with his eyes.

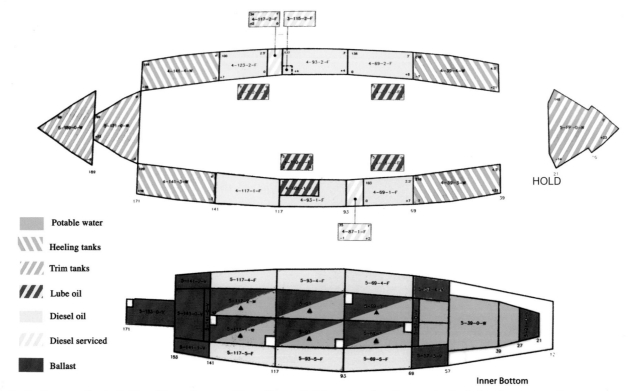

Potable water

Heeling tanks

Trim tanks

Lube oil

Diesel oil

Diesel serviced

Ballast

HOLD

Inner Bottom

Tank placement in the hold and lower bottom. The yellow and white stripped tanks contain the fuel to be consumed next.

"I am preparing for our fueling in Rogers City." He was searching the computer for the fueling checklist. Printed checklists serve to preserve the corporate memory which would otherwise be lost in the system of 3-year tours. The lists serve as educational tools to outline the steps in a task, as clocks to pace the work and, once completed, as a paper trail to verify the work. "There is a 24-hour check list that I am looking for. I have to hold three meetings and prepare the equipment before we can fuel." He had plenty of time to search the computer since we were still in Chicago, 30 hours from Rogers City. Later he told me that he found the checklist used at the last fueling as well as the one used decades ago. He found the old one interesting, with forgotten procedures that he revitalized. It made me wonder if the new *Mackinaw* would come with checklists already created by the design engineers, lists that would be modified with time.

Before we left Cheboygan the diesel fuel had been ordered. A crewman sounds every tank once a day by measuring the depth of the liquid in feet and inches. A computer program calculates the gallons of fuel onboard based on these soundings. One hundred and fifty thousand gallons had been ordered.

This, Pietrolungo explained, would fill us to 110% capacity. I thought I misunderstood. "No, he explained, we will fill to 110%. We want all we can carry when going into icebreaking. The heavier the boat, the better."

How much fuel does the *Mackinaw* hold? There are numerous fuel tanks onboard. Four large tanks hold around 40,000 gallons each and ten or more smaller tanks each hold around 15,000 gallons. In addition, there are two overflow tanks of 40,000 gallons each.

All of the large numbers on the *Mackinaw* numbed me. Forty thousand gallons, four hundred thousand gallons – once numbers get this large they lose meaning. To make it comprehensible I tried some analogies: a Ford F-150 truck with one 40,000-gallon fuel tank

Sounding a fuel tank. At some period the Mackinaw received fuel by truck at the Cheboygan dock. The trucks would run back and forth steadily for two 10-hour days.

could drive around the globe 32 times! Using all of the *Mackinaw's* fuel tanks, we could take a fleet of eight Ford F-150s around the world 32 times. Or, to think about it in another way, if you start driving when you are 16 years old and drive 1,000 miles a month until you are 76 years old, you will have burned roughly 40,000 gallons of fuel. It would take eight lifetimes to burn all of the fuel in the *Mackinaw*! Those same tanks will push the *Mackinaw* 1.6 times around

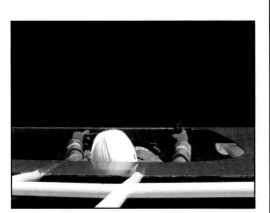

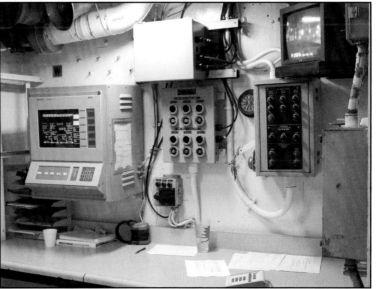

During fueling, crewmembers stand watch at every point of the fueling operation. The Damage Control room is one of the communications centers.

the globe if it doesn't bump into ice. Breaking ice burns fuel much faster, up to 600 gallons per hour. With a fill-up, the *Mackinaw* theoretically is good for a year; but it re-fuels twice each year, just before ice breaking and just after. On our trip to Chicago we were burning fuel that had been pumped aboard a year ago.

The gas stations are not on every corner. Rogers City is a nearby stop. Only three hours from Cheboygan, it has a big fuel storage tank and it won the government contract for fueling the *Mackinaw*. The *Mackinaw* will pay a modest $1.01 per gallon while at my gas station it is $2.10. But the *Mackinaw* is getting the lowest quality liquid fuel money can buy.

The *Mackinaw* was built with fuel processing equipment aboard. Each day's fuel is pumped through the processor from a main tank into the day-tank. This processor removes any water and debris, such as paint flakes, that might have settled into the tank. The boat runs from the clean day-tank.

We were going to fill two main fuel tanks and the two overflow tanks, putting us at 110% capacity. The crewman who ordered the fuel informed me that we had better not take on more than 150,000 gallons. If we exceed the order by 10% it would involve a ton of paperwork. We will take on 150,000 gallons.

Later I found Pietrolungo again. He was reviewing procedures and assignments. He had tentatively prepared the assignment sheet, putting 29 people at duty stations. He had produced a 3-deep redundancy for every job. We would back into the Calcite fueling dock in Rogers City with a port tie. Four crewmen would be in the fueling booth on the dock and the remaining 25 would be spread around the boat adjusting the fueling manifolds or taking soundings of levels. The first

St. Ignace's 47-footer came alongside. The crew were very cold. Notice the black face masks they all wore.

tank would be full when the fuel depth reached 19'8". This measurement would be taken using a steel tape much like a tape measure. It was important to keep a close eye on things during the five hours of fueling. The fuel would be coming aboard at 650 gallons per minute through a 4-inch pipe. One mistake could be disaster. In anticipation of fueling, spill retention booms were to be laid out, fire hoses faked nearby and all adjoining hatches locked down.

These procedures would be reviewed between the FOWK and the LLO in the first of the three meetings. The Coast Guard talks in acronyms. I asked Pietrolungo what was a meeting of a FOWK and an LLO. " It means I will meet with ENS Lawrence. I am the FOWK, fuel, oil and water king, and ENS Lawrence is the LLO, liquid load officer."

Pietrolungo was prepared as we left Chicago. But the weather dictates everything on a boat, and it is likely to change your plans, especially in November. November 15th is the date when the air temperature and water temperature differ the most in the Straits of Mackinac. A high temperature differential creates high winds. As we reentered the Straits we found that a gale-force, east wind was waiting for us. The *Mackinaw* turned her beam into 15-foot waves which caused our round-bottom boat to roll 27 degrees.

Fueling Safety Precautions for All Hands

1. Avoid contact with fuel and fuel vapors
2. No cigarette lighters with any fueling personnel
3. No spark producing tools shall be used during fueling
4. Quarterdeck shacks will not operate the heaters
5. Inspect your boots and make sure you don't have any metal stuck to them or any of the steel toe showing
6. No non-approved flashlights on the weather decks.
7. Any non-fueling personnel are prohibited from the main weather deck
8. You cannot go through the weather deck doors.
9. The smoking lamp will be extinguished during the entire evolution

Waiting for us in this cold rough sea was the 47-foot Coast Guard boat stationed in St. Ignace. They serve the Queen, doing whatever chores the large *Mackinaw* cannot do for itself. In this case, they were coming to take four crewmen off of the *Mackinaw* and put them ashore so they could drive to Rogers City and be prepared to take our lines when we docked.

The gale caused them to be stressed when they pulled alongside. A tardy crewman from the *Mackinaw* made things worse but the crew transfer took place without mishap. However, the gale continued. Productivity declines when people are chasing things around the cabins. Eating was the classic comedy skit of holding onto the plate, silverware and salt and pepper shakers. With four people at a table, each took responsibility for one edge of the teeter-totter tabletop. However, more serious was the arrangement at the fueling dock. The dock projects into the east. We would be tied up with our stern receiving the full force of the gale. It was time to anchor and wait out the storm.

As we rounded the Straits we knew we had come to safety in the lee of Bois Blanc Island. Two freighters were already anchored and one tug with a tow was circling. We pulled up, dropped anchor and rested for the night.

Anchoring had a mixed effect on the crew. Pietrolungo started pacing. He had his timing prepared so all the gear would be ready when we arrived at the dock, three hours cruising time from here. But now the timing was uncertain. How long would we be anchored? What should he be doing?

The captain also started pacing. We had been racing a freighter to the fuel dock. Fueling is a first-come, first-served operation. If we arrived after the freighter we would have to sit in the lake for 12 hours waiting our turn. The captain wanted to be there first.

A subtle shift in mood set in for the rest of the crew. We were within sight of homeport. Families were waiting. Couldn't we have pulled into port for the night? How long will we be sitting here?

The captain talked to the crew about the difference between rough weather while in transit and rough weather when trying to enter a narrow channel like the Cheboygan River or the Rogers City dock. We were not going to enter any narrow channels in this wind.

Daylight arrived and we were off in a dash. An hour down the lake the captain announced that we would fuel next. The freighter had fallen a day behind. Everyone smiled.

We arrived at Rogers City and slipped right up next to the dock. Our line handlers were waiting. They tied us up and then brought mail and supplies aboard. The fueling process began and we waited. The process was slow and careful. It was early evening and darkness had diminished our world to the lights of the Calcite plant. Suddenly there were lights from lakeward. A freighter was pulling in beside us. The slip is narrow and they glided slowly into place, about eight feet from our starboard rail.

This freighter was so close and we were so near our departure time that it seemed to me like a rude thing to do. Not long after the freighter arrived we were ready to leave. There was no room for us to pull away from the dock so we inched our way along. Our lines remained stretched to the dock and the dock hands carried them along and hooked them over the bollards at any sign that we were moving out from the dock. It took a long time to pull ourselves out from the dock. When we finally pulled away we again anchored for the night. Our engine room crews had been standing watch all day and needed rest.

Pietrolungo could rest. It would be four months before he acted as fueling king again.

The Mackinaw is a family-friendly ship. During ice breaking season the captain schedules "family days." A crew member's family can ride along for the day and see what the work is like. Here MK2 Pietrolungo is sharing breakfast with his son Hunter on the mess deck.

Jump ahead to the 2006 pre-Chicago trip when hurricane Katrina has just destroyed drilling platforms and refineries. Gas prices have sky-rocketed. At the same time the *Mackinaw* is heading into her final ice breaking season so it is her standard fill-up time. Because of the high fuel cost and the imminent decommissioning, the Coast Guard made the decision not to buy fuel. The empty tanks were cleaned and filled with water to achieve the desired ballast for ice breaking. The *Mackinaw* has headed down the road of no return.

Pietrolungo on the water and sewer system

by Pat Pietrolungo

"Being fuel and water king, I am in charge of knowing how much water is onboard. I keep a daily sheet on our potable water and our fuel.

"Our water systems reflect the technology of the 1940s. Today's larger ships have a reverse osmosis system where they can take water from the lake or the ocean and make potable water. We don't have that. So we have to store clean water in four tanks, around 40,000 gallons in all. We also have a 'sanitary water' system; this is lake water that is used for flushing toilets, for the boiler feeds and for the reefer compressor. This is pumped onboard with a pump located in #2 Space. Sometimes we have to conserve our use of water because we don't have enough storage space for the dirty water.

"We also have two dirty water systems on the boat, a greywater and a blackwater system. In the 1940s dirty water was just pumped overboard. Of course you cannot do that today so we always retain our sewage. We have permission to pump our greywater overboard while out on the lake. When we are in Chicago, Grand Haven and at home we retain all of our greywater, meaning the sink water and shower water. We have three greywater tanks with floats that turn the pumps on when the tanks are full. In Cheboygan we have a city sewage connection so we pump all of our dirty water over to the sewage connection. In Chicago and Grand Haven we don't have that luxury; we have to retain all of our water. We have three greywater tanks and two blackwater tanks. They fill quickly when you have nearly 100 people on board, crew and guests. When in Chicago we get a tank truck to haul it off. That costs about $700. Once we get out in the lake we can shift our greywater overboard through fittings in the side of the hull above the waterline.

"Our blackwater storage capability is our limiting factor for staying away from port. Our 7,300 gallons of blackwater storage suffices for about 14 days. We have a main sewage tank and then a new lower overflow tank that was added in 2002. The toilets work on a vacuum system. In the sewage flats a pump puts a vacuum on the sewage line itself. When someone operates the toilet button the pump sucks the sewage out. That causes the suction action that you feel as a rush of wind.

"It is interesting that this ship carries enough fuel to last a year but, even with the added sewage tanks, we can stay away from the docks no more than 14 days."

This is a photo of the forward propeller shaft alley in 1968. Originally the space had a beautiful geometric symmetry.

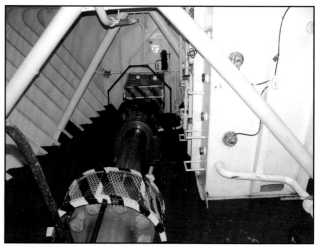

Today this same room houses a sewage tank along the starboard side, making the space more productive and less beautiful.

LTJG Andy Lawrence explains the sewage system.

"On *Mackinaw*, we use a vacuum sewage system. A vacuum pump creates a 10-15 inHG (inches of mercury) vacuum on an accumulator which is connected to the toilets by a piping system. The accumulator is always under a vacuum and discharges into the attached upper sewage tank, which is not under vacuum or pressure. This is actually vented through the ship's stack to the atmosphere, which is why it smells like sewage up there.

"When you press the flush button on the toilet, a valve opens to the vacuum piping and sucks the waste out of the toilet into the accumulator and sewage tank. Outside lake water fills the toilet bowl from our sanitary water system (it is called 'sanitary' water because it originally provided water for the showers too!).

"We have two sewage tanks. The main sewage tank, the upper one, holds 4,800 gallons and is directly attached to the accumulator and the sewage vacuum pumps. The second tank is an overflow tank, meaning that when the main sewage tank fills to halfway, we open a valve that lets the sewage flow into the lower tank located in the forward shaft alley. The lower tank's capacity is 2,300 gallons.

"To empty the sewage tanks we close off the vacuum piping going to the toilets and open valves going to the main deck (on either side of the fo'c'sle). We then use the sewage pumps to pump the sewage out of the tank to the deck and through hoses to the shore sewers. We also have piping and fittings designed to pump sewage overboard on the port side (when it was legal to do so on the Great Lakes), but we've locked the valves to prevent this from happening.

"The drain system for sinks, showers, and inside deck drains is an almost completely separate system. We call it the 'greywater system' or 'secondary drainage' (blackwater being raw sewage and greywater being drain water. Main drainage is for the bottom decks like engine rooms, motor rooms, and shaft alleys to remove water).

"Main drainage is an installed piping system that runs through all the lowest spaces in the ship, the engine rooms, motor rooms, pump rooms, and shaft alleys. This system can be operated in a flooding emergency using the ship's fire pumps (to suck from the space and pump overboard), or normally using one of three diaphragm pumps that moves water to our slop tank (we call it the 'slope tank'). From the slope tank we can pump the oily water to our Oily Water Separator which separates the oil from the water, sending the water overboard and the oil to a dedicated waste oil tank. When we change the oil on the engines we also send it to the waste oil tank. About once every other month we have a waste oil truck come to dispose of our waste oil.

"Our greywater system is broken up into three sections:

* the aft section is the galley, scullery, and first class showers and sinks--it gravity drains into #3 greywater tank, located in #1 Engine Room
* the middle section serves the crew's head showers and sinks--this section gravity drains into #2 greywater tank located in the Bow Motor Room
* the forward section serves the officers' sinks, officers' and chief's head showers and sink, and the forward berthing showers and sinks--it drains into #1 greywater tank located in the Starboard Pump Room.

"Each tank has a float operated pump that turns on when the tank gets full. The pumps are connected to a piping system so that the greywater can be directed to our upper sewage tank, overboard on the port or starboard side, or sent to a connection on the fo'c'sle. In port, we pump all the greywater to the sewage tank. Underway, we normally discharge the water overboard. This is illegal for new ships to do on the Great Lakes - the New *Mackinaw*, *Alder*, and *Hollyhock* all have enough tank storage for their greywater. If Old *Mackinaw* were prevented from discharging greywater into the lake, we would have to pull into port every 3 days to empty our tanks!."

Fire is a constant worry on any ship. A portion of the Mackinaw crew goes to firefighting school every summer in Toledo, where this photo was taken.

Tank Details

by Sandy Planisek

The *Mackinaw's* hull is pointed on both ends, an important design feature that allows the boat to be equally capable of making headway and sternway through broken ice. These pointed ends create peculiarly shaped interior spaces.

Boat designers are not dismayed by the space utilization problem. Fuel and water storage are always needed on a boat and the hull ends make good repositories. In the case of the *Mackinaw* the ends have been used to store ballast water, particularly in heel and trim tanks. The trim of the boat is the front-to-back aspect of the boat; the heel is the side-to-side aspect.

Heel and trim tanks are used to maximize fuel efficiency by leveling and re-leveling the boat. While it might seem that the boat would always sit level in the water, it does not. Adding loads on deck, consuming fuel, consuming potable water and filling sewage tanks all change the weight distribution in the boat. This displacement is monitored on the Heel & Trim Board in #2 Space which is filled with glowing glass indicators flanking large glass levels indicating the heel or trim of the boat. Dials

Heel Board in #2 Space. The two levels in the center allow for fine and gross leveling adjustments. Green lights mean the valve is open, red means closed.

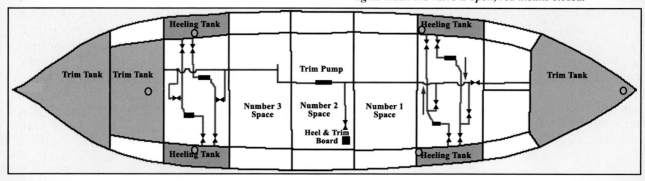

The heel and trim tank system contains 262,000 gallons of water, of which 3/4 is in the heeling system. The tanks are kept full and when the boat is heeled, the excess water rushes out of the yellow manhole covers. The quick action of the heeling system is possible because the water circulates in a 1-directional loop.

Crewmember monitoring a valve connecting the heeling tanks to the trim system. There are 14 valves in this system. The 15th, which connected the system to the deck, was removed some time ago.

off to the side indicate the water levels in the tanks.

The trim tanks are in the tips of the boat and the heel tanks are inward along the sides. These large water tanks are connected by pipes and outfitted with valves and pumps which can move the huge amounts of water in the tanks. Both systems can be used to level the boat. The heeling system also serves an icebreaking purpose. If the boat gets stuck up on ice, the heeling system can move 112,000 gallons of heeling water from side to side in just 90 seconds. Just like a car stuck in snow, rocking sometimes can help the boat break loose. And just like rocking a car, it takes an artist to get the process to work.

You can find the tanks by walking the main deck watching for manhole covers painted yellow with black stripes. These covers sit over the tanks. Workers enter the tanks through these covers and sloshing water escapes through the covers.

Tanks

by Sandy Planisek

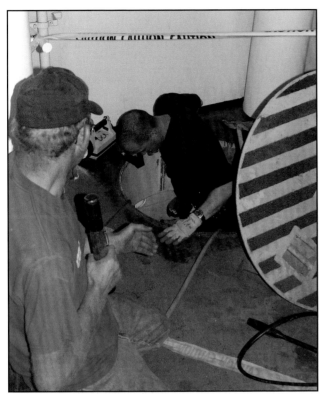

Entering the starboard, forward heeling tank through the manhole outside the wardroom

June 1st, near the end of spring "Charlie" or repair season, the spring maintenance work transforms the weatherworn icebreaker into the summer beauty queen. In 2005 she would be making her last public relations appearances at the ports of Lake Michigan. CDR McGuiness called and he wanted me to see these final repairs to the tanks onboard.

When I arrived at the dock she sparkled on the outside with fresh red and white paint, but I was here to visit her innards. Repairs and a fresh coat of paint were also being applied to the insides of her tanks.

LCDR Barner and LTJG Lawrence met me in the wardroom with coveralls. This was wet, messy business. I donned the gear and headed down the yellow-striped hatch marking the starboard, forward heeling tank. These are the tanks that slosh water back and forth to help her waddle back and off of any ice she might ride up on. It takes about 10 minutes to activate this system but when it gets rocking the crew can shift 112,000 gallons of water, about what an average household uses in 3 years, from one side to the other.

All of this water roaring back and forth wears on the paint and then wears on the steel of these tanks. Every few years the tanks need to be cleaned and repaired.

Inside the top level of the tank, the perforated bulkhead, called a swashplate, inhibits the development of waves in these tanks.

The view above is what they see through the holes at the left. The exterior of the boat is to the right in these photos.

The tanks are very large and are made up of several rooms. Bulkheads are perforated to allowed the water to run from one room to the next. The rooms are stacked three deep. The hatches connecting these spaces are small, the ladders steep, and the compartments plain. The only adornment is one meager float in the corner connected to depth sensors. No beauty here – just the beast.

We took our time, took lots of photos, and tried to understand how repairs were made in such a wet environment. Our enthusiasm must have been contagious because when we emerged we were offered another tour, a tour of the inside of the smokestack which had just been cleaned. We added protective booties for our shoes and headed up.

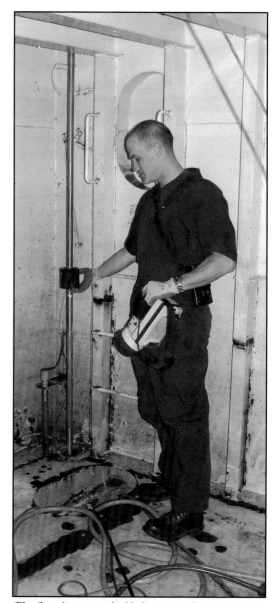

Here in the stern trim tank you can see the connecting rooms of the tank receding behind Lawrence's head. Moving water between trim tanks is a slower process and not an icebreaking maneuver.

The float has an embedded magnet. Its movement causes an electric current which sends a depth indication to the Trim Board. Notice the access hole to the next lower level of the tank near Lawrence's right foot.

Looking down into the lowest level in the trim tank you see a pit without a ladder. Lawrence enters and exits by pressing his body against the side walls. This view is down toward the keel.

The Stack

by Sandy Planisek

Getting into the stack is no easier than getting into the tanks. You crawl and slither under a steel overhang and wiggle through a tiny hatch. Once inside you can stand up and look unimpeded to the top. But, to my surprise, this isn't really a smokestack. I am inside a steel cowling loosely enclosing maybe a dozen vents heading up and out the top. The engines, the sewers, and other things I don't remember exit through this cowling.

The engines have not always performed as cleanly as they do now. Engine oil spews out of the stack and falls back down inside this cowl or onto the back deck. The back deck is cleaned regularly but the insides are cleaned less frequently. So a clean stack, after years of oil build-up, is still a dirty place.

Up the vertical ladder, maybe 20 feet, we emerge through a hatch onto a floor about four feet from the top of the stack. What an unexpected and wonderful place to gaze out over the scenery. It is an open-air room with a view. Numerous hatch covers and a chimney sweep's bristle-brush are the only obstacles to walking about in this space, the size of an office. Everything is painted black and on this June day the heat has attracted flying insects. It is a pleasant place but Lawrence says that normally the odor from the toilets is quite distracting. After a few snapshots our adventures inside the insides of this boat are over.

What a rare privilege this has been.

Protective booties and gloves keep off the soot.

The entry to the stack is under this overhang on 02 deck.

You enter the hatch which is about knee high. Once inside, the space opens around you with a maze of tubes running from below you to 20 or more feet above your head.

Dick Moehl exits out onto the floor inside the top of the stack. Lawrence is standing on one of the covers for the engine exhaust. These open automatically when exhaust is rising.

A vertical ladder leads to a mesh platform (bottom picture) where you cross over to another ladder which takes you up to the exit hatch (top picture) at the top of the stack. At the lower corners of this picture are the exhaust vents from two of the engines. Because of the exhaust heat they are insulated to this point. From here up they are bare rust-colored tubes.

The view up the Cheboygan River from the stack.

Master Chief

Master Chief Hamerle said the best opportunity for him has been to meet with Admiral Papp, Admiral Silva before him, and Bryan Clemons the District Nine Master Chief.   Master Chief Hamerle is at the top left, bottom left is Admiral Papp, central is MC Bryan Clemons, and at far right is CDR McGuiness

by Sandy Planisek

When you walk into a place containing 80 people some will stand out and others will not, some are flamboyant, some are quiet. On the *Mackinaw* there are a lot of quiet people and it took me a while to meet them. One who found me first was Master Chief Hamerle. He sought me out and asked if I would like to watch and photograph a fire drill. "Sure!" First he took me to the lockers so that I was in position when the alarm went out. I was able to watch the crew don their ensembles and answer to muster. People came rushing in, scrambling to put on gear, while others were searching for missing persons. About the time the crew was dressed Master Chief took me to where the pretend fire was supposed to be happening. He stood me in a corner and then said, "OK now we are having a fire," and then he turned out the lights. I stood in the dark for what seemed a long time and then the firemen arrived. It was actually sort of comical since I really couldn't see anything. After it was over I learned that the space held

the back-up batteries to jump-start the ship if needed. This area and the kitchen are likely fire spots.

From then on I recognized Master Chief and got to talk to him regularly. He is a quiet, serious man. He is extremely well spoken and he formulated complete sentence answers every time, something almost no one can do. He was very thoughtful about Coast Guard leadership policy issues.

Here is Master Chief Charles Hamerle speaking about his life on the *Mackinaw*.

"Before I joined the Coast Guard I worked in a diesel engine shop. I was basically a grease monkey, cleaning parts. So when I joined, I had some experience working on engines. Coming out of boot camp I was inclined to go bosun mate.

My company commander was a bosun mate and I was impressed with his career and what he had accomplished. But when I went to my first unit, Support Center Kodiak, I was assigned to the public works division. I became friends with electricians and machinery technicians and damage control men. They gave me a favorable impression of the MK rate, machinery technician. MKs are at almost every unit in the Coast Guard so I knew my opportunities would be widest in that rate.

"The unit that I was at before this was a land billet, Cape Disappointment. It was a category five job. People in those jobs choose last in the assignment process. The *Mackinaw* and Group Ketchikan were the two choices remaining to me. I had an ill mother who prevented me from going to Ketchikan; they didn't have the medical facilities that she needed. So I took orders to *Mackinaw* and brought my mother here to Cheboygan.

"When we are at Special Sea Detail I am back at main control. I am there with the warrant officer, the senior electrician, the engineer officer. We are back there about three-quarters of the time. Should any problem arise, there are enough people to remain there so that the expert can go to the main trouble spot. Other times my work place is in this office. I mostly do administrative work: working on parts orders, working on training, doing administrative remarks entries for personnel, whether they be positive entries for their record or negative entries.

Fire training onboard is done regularly.

Paperwork is a big part of all the senior crewmembers' jobs.

"On occasion they have what is called a damage control college. That typically happens in June or July when we have a lot of new people onboard who are working on their damage control qualifications. The damage control men will come up with curriculum and a schedule. Later, after transfer season, we get a few new people, one or two at a time, and training is just a continuing process, not very formal.

"All new crewmembers make drawings of ship systems, of the fire mains, for example. We have pumps down in the engine rooms, all the way up to the weather decks. It is important for all of the crew to understand where all of those pipes are, where all of the cutout valves are, so that should we have a fire we know how to operate the system. If we have damage to the system we will know how to work around the damage. I am on the damage control training team. The engineering officers have typically allotted time to hold damage control drills. When we are informed of those training availabilities we draft the drills. We have meetings to discuss how the drill is expected to go, then we hold the drills.

"Work force turn is one of our biggest problems. We lose one third to one half of our crew every year and it can be difficult to manage the training, getting the new people up to speed, maintenance of the old ship, and the needs of our people. Everyone has the need to get away from the ship and have some quality leave. Balancing training, maintenance, and that time for them is difficult. The newest people in the Coast Guard are typically here from six months to a year. It usually takes three to four months before they are qualified in their positions. Depending on which school they are waiting to go to and how long the wait, that is how much time we have to use them in their capacity. I understand that the new icebreaker will have no engineering non-rates, people just out of boot camp waiting to go to a technical school. That is a good idea because otherwise it places a burden on the command to get these people trained and then we lose them shortly after to a school. It is much better, I think, to get them trained in their technical jobs and then have them come in when they are going to spend three or four years. The return on the investment is better that way.

"Being involved in mentoring and leading 70 enlisted people has been a real educational experience for me. I have learned a lot about senior enlisted management and leadership. I feel better prepared to tackle that position again. I am eligible to retire now but I have applied for a job at headquarters working with the new integrated deep-water project in Washington.

"The engineering office is where senior engineers get together almost every day to discuss the condition of the plant, the plans for maintenance of the plant, and to discuss personnel issues. Often we meet here to vent a little bit.

We might be frustrated at the way the schedule changes or the way plans for maintenance are now changed because of some operational need. As senior engineers and personnel managers we can come in and close the door with the sign that says knock before entering. But the engineering officers' stateroom is where I will meet with the main propulsion assistant, my boss.

"The people who don't make it on the *Mackinaw* are those who are all about themselves, so they don't have a good view for the future. This is a 3-year job for most of us. This ship is one of the best-kept secrets in the Coast Guard as far as being a ship underway. You can point to a lot of days spent away from homeport but a lot of those days are spent in Chicago or Marinette or any number of ports.

"The Coast Guard was a great deal for me being as my high school grades were not particularly good. My parents did not have the money to send me to college. Not having a good idea of what I wanted to do with my life, the military provided me with a career, structure, discipline, so even if I left with only four years I would have been much better prepared for adult life. As it turns out, I did well almost my entire career, almost all of my jobs. I've done well in the advancements. So here I am Master Chief. When I was a young fireman I never thought I would become a Master Chief.

The Mackinaw crew practicing with a real fire at the Toledo school.

George Keefer

"If you are going to be an engineer then school is very important. I went to six different engineering schools. The best advice I have for a little kid is work on the study habits, work on being able to concentrate, on getting your homework done, work on being able to talk to your teachers about how well you are doing and what you can do to do better. Earn grades that might get you into college."

Master Chief Hamerle speaking about resource allocation

"The new *Mackinaw* will have two main Caterpillar engines with alternating current generators. We have six main Fairbanks Morse engines with direct current generators. Alternating current generators were not available for main propulsion in 1943. The control systems will be much more modern. The maintenance plan for them will be much different. I believe they plan to use contractors for all of the challenging maintenance aspects, for major repairs, for extensive rebuilds.

Fire fighting school in Toledo is the best possible training. Not everyone gets to go every year, but those who go learn very important skills.

"Here we do most of the major repairs ourselves. For an engineer one of the pleasures of being on this ship is that we are able to tear an engine down completely ourselves. Only occasionally do we call for a factory rep to stand-by during the rebuild. We are able to do all of the work ourselves.

"However this responsibility is not always fun. We were scheduled to go to the Chicago-to-Mackinac sailboat race and we had major engine repairs to complete. This was mid-summer when people should be getting ready for their new deployment and enjoying some time with their families. But because of the time constraints, the crew was working very late into the night to get these repairs accomplished. There was a great sense of satisfaction when it was all done, a great sense of pride, but the family suffers. As a salaried Coast Guard crewman there is no financial benefit. You can get a commendation but you are not going to get any overtime pay for working 14-hour days.

"The new *Mackinaw* crew will be able to have their down time when the ship has its down time. The contractor will be working on the ship while the crew is preparing for their deployments. That will be the good side of it. The bad side is you will have a Coast Guard engineer here that will be an

Here MK1 is teaching numerous young MKs about rebuilding an engine.

administrative contracting expert and will be much less of a hands-on machinery repair person.

"One of the bad things is the Coast Guard assigns someone to a station for two or three years. They just have time to learn the engines. They might keep good records on what they have done but still they leave with all the corporate knowledge. The good thing about a contractor is that you won't have repetitious mistakes caused by a constant stream of new people. You would hope a contractor would work in the area for many years. He will be fully aware of *Mackinaw's* history.

"Throughout the last 20 years they have threatened decommissioning of the *Mackinaw* several times and each time the ship took a dive in maintenance. We are still finding backyard repairs that we have to correct. This crew hasn't fallen into that trap. We are maintaining the ship as if we might be told that we have another five or 10 years to go, in case the new *Mackinaw* isn't meeting expectations

"The engines are challenging because they are so old and so worn. The fuel control racks have a lot of slop in them. It is a very time consuming job to tear apart the front cover

Sometimes time becomes short and the experienced crew have to finish the job. MK1 John Cripe

and get that whole rack replaced, not to mention expensive. Today the engines responded the best I have seen yet. In the past any major speed changes required that you adjust the air pressure to the engines so they matched in output. Today both engines were coming up nice and even. We have a good bunch of senior engineers on board, Petty Officers Holt, Lowery, and Short and through their insight and foresight we have the engines performing very well.

"I'm sorry that *Mackinaw* is going away. I think as a platform and as an icebreaker she is going to be real hard to beat. She cuts a nice wide track and her hull is strong. Her running gear is strong. Her engines aren't as easy to maintain as we like but, with new engines and refitting for crew comfort and safety, she could serve another 20 or 30 years. But to do any significant refitting they would want to remove the cork insulation, which is held on with asbestos glue. The refit would cost nearly what the new *Mackinaw* is going to cost, but the savings in personnel is a tough cost to beat. Between the *Acacia* and *Mackinaw* the new *Mac* will allow the CG to shift about 65 personnel to places where they are needed more.

"The Lake Carriers Association was a big sponsor of the new *Mackinaw* so I assume they signed off on her design. When breaking heavy ice for the larger ships we have to make two passes to give the ice a place to go. The new *Mackinaw* will cut a narrower track but faster, turn around quicker, and make that second pass faster. Where the new cutter is going to lose is when you are breaking for a smaller ship, like the tug *Michigan*. It is able to fit right in our track without any problem. We don't have to make a relief track. That is where you are going to run into problems with the new, narrower *Mackinaw*.

"One of the more special things about *Mackinaw* is the love of her past crews. We just had the 60th reunion cruise and dinner at the Golddust Ball Room. There was a roomful of people who came from all over the country to be here. We don't see that in any other ship. Every ship I have been on has been decommissioned. This is one of the newer ships I have been on. All of these older ships have no reunion committees, no reunion cruise. Pretty much the crews just go quietly away. *Mackinaw* is so special people want to stay involved with her."

The new Mackinaw entering the Cheboygan River for the first time. A crowd of well wishers lined the pier.

CDR Joe McGuiness, Commanding Officer Coast Guard Cutter Mackinaw

CDR is the military abbreviation for Commander, a military rank. If CDR McGuiness gets promoted he will become a Captain. Commanding Officer is a job description and says that CDR McGuiness is the top officer on the ship. In the crew's everyday conversation he is referred to as the captain. Once I heard him referred to as "the old man," an antique military expression. He refers to himself as skipper. This interview was held in February 2005.

Why did you choose to serve on the *Mackinaw*?

"Mackinaw was my first choice, plain and simple. *Mackinaw* is a one of a kind, a big, heavy, powerful tool. You know you are going to have good work to do with *Mackinaw* every year. I love the icebreaking mission because no matter where we take *Mackinaw* people are happy to see us. You hear the old timers talk about it all of the time on the radio. A few weeks ago we were working in the Straits of Mackinac and there were three ships stuck. We made our first radio call and we heard two of the masters talking to each other on a working channel saying, 'Great, here comes *Mackinaw*. We will finally get out of here. It is great to see that old thing up here because when she shows up you know you are going to move.' It is just a great, great tool. You feel really good doing your work.

"In the Coast Guard, when cutters are doing law enforcement missions or search-and-rescue missions the hull of the ship becomes transportation to the mission. You use the cutter for transportation. Then you put small boats over for a boarding party to do the work. With *Mackinaw* you work the ship. I am still fascinated by physically moving the ship. Relatively speaking, it is a large Coast Guard cutter operating in small, confined waterways, using tremendous amounts of power to work within feet of shoals, or rock walls, or docks, or other ships. If you like that kind of work, there is no substitute for a tour on the *Mackinaw*."

Is the *Mackinaw* what you expected?

"The boat ended up being what I expected and more. I had a Great Lakes tour on a 140 (one of the smaller icebreakers) a few years ago. After we had worked for three or four days and had exhausted our abilities, I watched *Mackinaw* come down and cruise right through things. I thought she must be really good but I don't think I had a concept of just how capable the ship really is. The designers must have been mad geniuses who sat down with paper and conceived what *Mackinaw* should be. She is a purpose-built icebreaker for the Great Lakes. They had to make fewer compromises when they built *Mackinaw*. So you end up sailing a ship that is really good at its mission. It is very rewarding."

Entering the locks is a close operation, especially when the ice in the locks is pushing you around.

What are its particular strengths?

"Size! Displacement! Power produced in a high torque fashion! It is not just horsepower, but your ability to turn the propellers. Simplicity! There is a lot of complexity to it but it is a simple machine by today's standards. Robustness! We can take a lot of damage. She has systems and back-up systems and engines and extra engines that allow you to continue to conduct the mission while you do repairs on yourself. But in the end, there is no replacement for displacement. Ice breaking is a momentum game. Mass and velocity are the two components of momentum. Velocity you can build into any ship but *Mackinaw* has mass, exceptional mass.

"I think of what makes a good icebreaker in two ways. First is your ability physically to break ice. For 62 years *Mackinaw* clearly has proved that she can do that. Second, and perhaps more importantly, is the ability to move commerce. Can the freighters move behind you? We could go out with a laser beam and cut a ¼ inch swath through six feet of ice. That would be breaking ice but no freighter could follow. *Mackinaw* breaks a swath that is at least 75 feet wide and sometimes, if we have speed on, it is considerably wider. If it is as wide or wider than the freighter's hull the freighter will come along behind us just as nice as you please."

The tradition of the crew walking around the boat on the ice goes way back. Notice that the boat does not carry the Coast Guard stripe in this photo.

What about the new *Mackinaw*?

"I'd love the chance to be the first skipper on the new boat. It is a very different tool and it is a fascinating tool. They are going to have to break ice in different ways than we break ice. Figuring out how to use that tool to do the job will be a blast. Nobody will have written a book on how to move commerce with the new ship. I'd love the chance to go out and figure it out. It is the difference between pick-up trucks. I drive an F250, a full size pick-up truck. But I keep looking at the Ford Rangers, the smaller ones. There a few times each year that that F250 is really good, when I want to take the whole family camping and we are towing a boat and we've got the dog with us. We've got all that gear and everything goes in the F250. Or there are a couple of days when we will be really hauling firewood out of the woods. Then there is no substitute for the F250. But 94 days out of 100 what I do with that F250 is get groceries, I pick the kids up, and I drive myself to work. Do I need an F250? On those camping days or wood hauling days could I make two trips with the Ford Ranger and not pay the extra price for the F250, not pay the extra fuel for the F250? Maybe someday I'll try that Ford Ranger. I'd like to try that new ship.

CDR McGuiness in the captain's chair overseeing his crew while they are backing during the icebreaking work.

The new Mackinaw headed out of the Cheboygan River on buoy tending training in the spring of 2006.

"We have an OT&E plan for the new ship. We are in the military so we have to have an acronym. Operation, test, and evaluation plan. The general concept is that the old ship will go out and move commerce during the overlap year which takes the pressure off of the Coast Guard to do operational things with the new ship. We can go out and do engineering tests with it. We think we know what we built, we think we know what the model is, now let's take the real ship out there in ice and find out, will it break ice? We can outfit it with probes, sensors, and computer equipment then find some ice to run it in. What's the vibration? What are the stresses? Is the hull flexing? Is the hull safe and stiff? Will it have good longevity? That's the plan for 2006. I have either been

sailing icebreakers in the lakes or working with management in the icebreaking operations for seven or eight winters. The more I know, the less I can tell you about what an average year is. So we have this great plan. Now we are going to see what Mother Nature gives us. What if we don't get any ice? What if we get the worst ice year in the last 50 years? That would be a great test for the new ship.

"The good news about the design of the new ship is we aren't starting from scratch. She has some custom adaptations and some new technology for the U.S. Coast Guard. But mariners have been using icebreakers of that general size and that general design in Europe for 20 years now. But she

Being the last captain on the last icebreaking mission generates considerable notoriety.

John Wagner

The old Mackinaw laying 30 miles of tracks in Whitefish Bay

is new to us and we are interested to see how she is going to perform or how we are going to have to adapt our operations to move commerce here. I don't worry about the ultimate success of it. Ultimately I am quite confident that she will be a successful ship. I'd just like to be the guy that gets to try to figure it out."

But you have the challenge of trying to hold this old one together.

"Yes, that has its days. The people who designed it were marvelously competent architects and engineers. One of the challenges for the old ship is the deployment cycle where the crew members come on for two or three years and then go to their next assignment. I think we can still be learning about the old ship at the end of our third year. The more we learn, the more we figure out about all of the valves, all of the piping, all of the systems, the more we realize that they knew exactly what they were doing when they built this. Sometimes we have a plain old physical problem; we snapped something inside an engine or we broke a piece of machinery. But we also have a lot of problems where we don't thoroughly

The captain's bed is against the front wall of the ship and he says the insulation isn't that good. Notice that there are three telephones within arm's reach. He is pointing to his bookcase which is full of manuals and one leisure reading book, Titanic. When asked why he has this book, he said it is good to remember that no ship is unsinkable.

understand how to operate the machine because it didn't come with any manuals, or if it did, they disappeared a long time ago. Your knowledge over three years is the knowledge of what you dealt with over three years and how you solved the problems. It is not necessarily a complete set of knowledge about how to operate the ship. The more we learn, the more amazed we are. We had a particular problem all of last year and it turns out we had the plant set up in a different way than the designers intended. When we realized that, we solved the problem."

It seems like a lot of people are using checklists from the past. Did the boat come with these checklists?

"Definitely not. Or if it did, they disappeared a long time ago. The theory of a checklist is that they are modified and improved by each crew. Check lists can do two things. They are great tools if you have a complex process to go through with relatively new personnel. To get the ship underway we

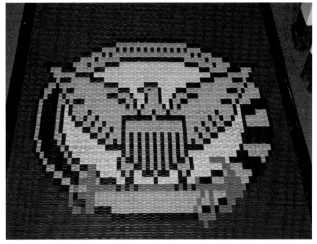

The entry to the captain's quarters is marked by this colorful floor mat.

AFTER WE SHIFT POWER:

BM _____ UNCOVER AND TEST SEARCHLIGHTS, ALL NAVIGATION LIGHTS AND ICE LIGHTS. WARM THEM UP AND WAIT FOR THE TEN-MINUTE TIMER TO IGNITE THEM.

BM _____ SET UP VHF/ FM RADIOS

BM_____ ENERGIZE 73 RADARS

BM_____ ENERGIZE THE 69 RADAR

BM_____ SET HEADING ON 73 MASTER RADAR

BM_____ MAKE POSITION COMPARISON USING ALL MEANS OF NAVIGATION. (LOG YOUR GYRO BEARINGS AND RADAR RANGES, DEPTH, AND THE LATITUDE AND LONGITUDE OF EACH METHOD OF OBTAINING A FIX IN THE BEARING BOOK.)

BM_____ POST RADAR RANGE ERROR AT EACH REPEATER, INCLUDE DTG AND THAT THE ERROR APPLIES TO RANGE SETTINGS OF 3NM OR LESS

BM _____ OBTAIN GYRO ERROR, LOG IN NAV DATA SHEET

BM_____ ENSURE THAT GYRO ERROR IS WRITTEN NEAR ALL GRYO REPEATERS (HELM, CONNING STATIONS AND AFT STEERING)

BM_____ POST CURRENT WATER LEVELS IN CONNING STATIONS

BM_____ ENSURE THE INTERCOMS ARE WORKING

BM_____ ENSURE PYRO LOCKER IS UNLOCKED (CONTACT BMOW)

BM _____ OBTAIN LATEST WEATHER FORECAST, POST ON THE WEATHER BOARD

A section of the check list used by the bridge to get underway.

have a bridge check-off list. So, you put all of the jobs on the check-off list and 99 times out of 100 you will get the ship successfully underway. If you want to talk to someone on the radio, the radio will be on and will be on the right channel because it is on the checklist. The trouble with a checklist is that after a while nobody questions it. You stop thinking because you get into the checklist mode. I'm not going to think about how to lite off an engine or think about the problem we are having, I am simply going to go through what the checklist tells me. If you follow the checklist accurately and you still have a problem, why? That is where it is fun. You get to be not only a technician but also an artist. You get to think through a problem, its causes and its solutions."

What is your most memorable experience on the boat?

"There are a lot of them. I have had so much fun. Mechanically, the days we tried to move the *Edgar B. Speer* by ourselves. It was fun watching the crew come together focused on a specific mission. They applied all of this machinery simultaneously, from the giant old towing machine, to all of the engines, to all of the shafts, and really got to see what the ship could do. Everybody focused on the same goal. That was a neat shipboard experience.

Command Philosophy

OUR MISSION
We move ships when no one else can.

YOUR RESPONSIBILITY
Keep yourself and your ship Semper Paratus.
Conduct yourself with honor, respect, and devotion to duty.
Leave yourself, your ship, and your shipmates better than you found them.

MY RESPONSIBILITY

I will guide you as you carry out your responsibilities
and accomplish our mission.

J. C. McGuiness

George Keefer

Growing up on the Mackinaw

A poem to CDR McGuiness who is referred to as #12 and BRB is his big red boat, the *Mackinaw*, by retired Commander Jim Sutherland. Semper Paratus is the Coast Guard moto meaning Always Prepared.

An exercise in the art of observation will reveal the following:

Watching #12 and his BRB,
we know he is very quiet,
starts early,
has everybody trained and in place,
then very slowly
and very carefully
he gets "underway"
without a fuss or frazzle,
does the job completely,
thoroughly,
safely. And
with a great sense of
pride and accomplishment,
he puts her to bed to be
SEMPER PARATUS
another day.

"Personally, the things that are the most rewarding are the growth you get to see in the new folks that come to the ship. Lots of people who sail with us have never been to sea before. Crossing the brow onto your first cutter is a pretty daunting psychological task. You don't know anything about this new life, this new culture, this new ship, this new crew you are joining. Some of them grow from very apprehensive, very unsure individuals to competent leaders aboard the ship, never mind just competent crew, competent leaders who really find themselves and start to believe in themselves, believe in their ability to do things. It is really rewarding to set up the workplace that allows for that kind of growth, that allows people to find their place, to grow into leadership roles. In a very short time, a year or two, they become the mentor or teacher for the new people who come on."

What is the most difficult part of your job?

"Difficult can be different from unpleasant. The unpleasant is when positive leadership efforts don't bear fruit and you have to cross over into negative leadership accountability for negative actions. We have had our share of that in the last 18 months. Nobody enjoys it, not from the captain to the person being punished. You always wonder, was the person a troublemaker when they showed up at the ship or did the ship teach them to be a troublemaker? That is what is always in my mind. Ultimately everybody is responsible for his or her own behavior."

Learning while on the Mackinaw

the wrong time. You are playing the bad guy when you set the special sea detail and get everybody up to go through a narrow passage at 2 am, even though everybody would rather sleep and we have been through here successfully before. But when you say you will be a ship captain you say you will take those responsibilities."

What duties does the commanding officer do vs. the executive officer (exec or XO)?

"Traditionally, the execs run the ship while in port and the skipper runs the ship while underway. In the ideal world the captain has very little work to do in port. Every day XO St. John and I talk together for 45 minutes to discuss what is going to be done on a series of objectives. Commander St. John, as the exec, goes off and accomplishes those things. A lot of people think the captain is the guy on the wheel while underway. But on a big ship it is usually not that way. Usually we have trained a series of people to be on the wheel and be on the throttles as the deck watch officer of the ship. The captain is trying to figure out where the ship needs to be three hours from now, or tomorrow. My typical day underway is burning up a cell phone, a lot of communication, a lot of organization, and a lot of developing cooperative plans that the ships and shipping companies buy into. So I spend most of my time communicating with people who are off the ship. Then once we agree to that plan, I bring it back to our ship and say here is our part of the big plan. We need to be underway at this time, in this spot."

How do you interact with your bosses?

"Captain Mike Hudson is my immediate boss in Cleveland,

What is the most difficult part of the job?

"I think the difficult part of the job is keeping everyone focused on the essentials when we all start to get tired. When you have been in the river seven, eight, nine, ten days in a row it is very easy to get overly familiar with the river. When you are on your first trip up the St. Marys River you can't believe how tight the river is, how close it is, how perfectly turns have to be executed. You're as tight as a drum your first trip up the river. By your 4th, 5th, 6th, 7th, 8th, 9th, 10th, 25th, 30th trip up the river you are very relaxed. Nothing has changed about the danger of the river. You're just more familiar, to the point where maybe you are overly familiar with it. So keeping people focused on the very basic things when we are all getting a sense of over-familiarity is a difficult task because people stop believing the job is difficult. That's when something bad is going to happen. You'll lose an engine while you are coming through a turn or you'll lose steering, and because you haven't set yourself up to be the safest you can be, now you find yourself in a compromised position. So I am ordering people to do more work than they think is necessary. That is about having experience, having seen a ship lose power in a turn, having seen an engine fire at exactly

The cult of the Mackinaw was recognized early in her career. Folks lined up to tour this majestic vessel.

then Admiral Robert Papp the District Commander. They come two or three times a year for different events. I try to get them out for a ride on the *Mackinaw*. They get to see snapshots of the ship, similar to what you get to see. It is very independent work and I have a lot of ultimate responsibility for the decision making. But a lot of it is collaborative and consultative too. Part of making a good decision as a ship's skipper is making sure your boss is comfortable with that decision and will back you up should it be questioned. Icebreaking is a closed community. If you are a good icebreaker it becomes known. A good ship is in the right place at the right time with the river ready to go for the transit. A bad ship is showing up behind the freighter it is supposed to escort, or it is leading them into places that they can't get out of or it has a bunch of issues. It is a small enough group that if you are doing things right and you are moving ships people know it. They talk about it and they just plain old appreciate it. And if you are not, then there is the other edge of that sword too."

Admiral Papp commented on the number of people who re-request to be on the *Mackinaw*.

"We did have a lot of folks ask to extend, particularly for *Mackinaw*'s last year. It is a compliment to the ship; it is a good place to work. Senior Coast Guard leaders want the Coast Guard to be a good place to work. There has to be a balance between the Coast Guard and the Coast Guardsman. We provide enough pay, a good enough life style, and what the Coast Guard really provides is good work to do. You don't have to rescue many people at sea before you decide this is pretty good work. I like this. This is not a job where you worry that you sold someone something that they didn't need or couldn't afford. This is very nourishing work.

"One of the things that fascinates me about *Mackinaw* is the cult of *Mackinaw*. Why do so many old sailors stay with it, come back to visit it. I know of no other cutter that is like that. Not only do they come back, but we had hundreds last year, sold out the ballroom. They are so happy to be here. There must be something about this ship. It was a good part of their lives, particularly if they were not career Coast Guard folks. They were part of something big, an element of adventure, an element of operating outside your comfort zone learning new things, operating with people who become your lifelong friends. They are not only being part of something bigger than themselves, but something that they know at their core is good. It is humanitarian, good for the country, good for your neighbors."

What else would you want to say to someone visiting this door?

"If they were touring *Mackinaw* I would want to tell them, 'Welcome aboard. You are standing on one of the longest serving, most revered and loved, truly competent and

awesome icebreakers we have ever built and probably ever will build. You are on the *Mackinaw*, you are on the real deal. She may be old and she may have run out of parts, but we are not building a new ship because the old one couldn't do the work. Boy could the old one work.'

"I would wish that everybody who comes to tour the *Mackinaw* could have ridden *Mackinaw* in March when we go above the locks for the first time and we put those throttles down and you watch all that heat and power come up out of the stack and watch the wake behind. And no matter what ice is in front of you, the ship just starts to move up on top of the ice and breaks that first path. You realize what a neat amazing, amazing ship it really was - is - probably always will be. For 63 years, from World War II, all the way through Vietnam, through the 50s, the 60s, the 70s, this ship has kept the economy of our grandparents, our parents, and us more competitive, kept the raw materials flowing down, things we never think about. When you buy a car you never think about where the steel came from. *Mackinaw* is a big part of getting that steel made.

"But when you stand on her decks and she is quiet, that is not what she is about. She is about being out at sea, all those engines hooked up to all those motors, all those propellers. She is about crashing through and making that first path so other ships can follow. It is just a lot of fun. I wish everybody could have seen it."

Welcome Aboard!

"Nourishing Work"

The Mackinaw in her white days backing down to lead the Edwin H. Gott out of trouble. The Mackinaw is aided by one of the 140-foot icebreakers.

The End

Now the book is done. I have explained what I saw and learned. There is much more to say but . . .

Now I must answer the question I posed at the outset. What is the story of the *Mackinaw* for me?

I have been aboard many times and know many of the crew. Yet the next time I step aboard I still will be entering a foreign land. And like a traveler in a foreign land, I will never be completely at home. The culture is strange to me and the people unique.

In this city-state the crewmembers have different traditions, mores, and even work schedules. They have their own language with a unique vocabulary peppered with acronyms. They have their own fashions decorated with patches of cloth and ribbons. They read each other's clothing enough to distinguish each other's rank, expertise, and experience. I never learned to decipher the subtle codes. The range of traits is narrow: the people are all young, smart, agile, and friendly. There are 10 men to every woman. Their illnesses are those caused by accident. The largest use of free time is spent in learning. Immigration and emigration from the boat are routine. Bundled together this makes a high energy, temporary society. How different from my world.

Most strangely, these people live and work inside a machine. Granted they occasionally come to the surface to work but life is centered in the interior. These people are the power of the machine and the slaves to it. They understand the machine; they bandage its wounds, modernize its systems, and fuel its engines. They are its eyes and its brain. They feed its heart and keep its arteries cleaned. They thrive on their relationship with it.

Amazingly, when these foreigners step off of the machine they turn into ordinary Cheboyganites. They assume all the traits of the local culture. Which is the masquerade and which the reality? Perhaps some are one and some the other.

I worry about some of them. Their formative years are spent being part of something larger than themselves. They are important, part of a critical team. What happens to them after 20 years? What happens to them when they retire, at a young age, to a routine life doing mundane things?

I have been working on the *Mackinaw* book, feverishly trying to get it done before the boat is decommissioned. It has been an interesting six months. The new *Mackinaw* arrived after having tested her hull strength in Grand Haven. From my armchair it seems she had a classic shallow-water, high-speed collision. But she arrived in Cheboygan with a freshly painted, dimpled bow on the appointed day, albeit, not at the appointed hour. She took her time, crept into the harbor and docked about 45 minutes late to cheers from the frozen crowd. The old *Mackinaw* bellowed out a Great Lakes salute and the new *Mackinaw* tooted back. The festivities that night at the Golddust Ball Room were less than festive. The new crew had to face the worries about both the size of the new vessel and her accident. The crew of the old *Mackinaw* had to face the realization that her life was over.

The countdown began that night. The old *Mackinaw* is now proceeding through all of the "lasts." I was fortunate enough to be aboard for her last transit upbound through the locks. In her honor there were cameramen everywhere, including the sky above, shooting her last workout. But Mother Nature did not provide a lot of ice, just a moderate amount. And the Canadian vessel *Samuel Risley*, who locked up with *Mackinaw*, paid her respects by following behind for half a day and then proceeded to easily pass us at Gros Cap Reefs Light.

Now there are only 40 days until decommissioning and the future of the *Mackianw* still changes daily. The Icebreaker Mackinaw Maritime Museum group is trying to arrange her retirement. Plans are still uncertain. Will she go off to Baltimore, the old-age home for Coast Guard ships, or will she flourish again in her role as a museum ship?

What I know for certain is that I will be at the decommissioning and I will be in tears. This boat without its crew will never be truly alive again. Every time I head back to the boat, it is to see someone, not to see the steel plate or exciting engines. The boat is a concert of people under the hands of a respected and capable director.

Long live the memory of the *Mackinaw*!

Putting on the final touches

A Tale of Two Guards

by LTJG Molly Killen

I often hear the expression "Old Guard" used with a tone of veneration in a description of some crusty old salt, or a wistful tone in reminiscences of days of yore. "New Guard" is more commonly accompanied by derision, as it denotes people and policies that offend said crusty old salts. While I've yet to see definitions of these terms in print, I believe I have made direct observations of the various manifestations of these opposing forces in people, practices, and equipment.

A Tale of Two MPAs. Our previous Main Propulsion Assistant was 100% Old Guard. First, he was old; stereotypical Crusty Warrant Officer. He prowled about, brandishing a wicked scowl. When he was really angry, the three hairs remaining on top of his head stood on end. Then there was his sense of decor. His stateroom was luxuriously appointed with . . . a Fairbanks Morse calendar. "Hey, look . . .Main Diesel Engine #3 is Miss June!" The conning officers were plagued with a fear of his bark over the squawk box: "Watch your amps!!"

Then came the day when our new MPA arrived. A Volkswagen bus pulled into the MPA parking spot, and out stepped a man literally half the age of his predecessor, and in a tie-dyed t-shirt. The stunned onlookers were greeted with, "How you cats doin'?" We have yet to hear an admonishment over the squawk. While no less knowledgeable or effective, our new MPA is just too mellow for that sort of thing. If he did find occasion for such action, we estimate it would sound something like, "Think you cats could calm down up here?"

A Tale of Two Coffee Drinkers. The XO is profoundly Old Guard in at least one respect: his coffee preferences. Or, I should say, preference. Straight, black, and lots of it. No frills, no additives. Just plain, coffee-flavored coffee beans from somewhere in South America.

My own inclinations are best understood when illustrated.

[Right after lunch]

Me: "By your leave, Cap'n?"

Cap'n: "Sure. Foofoo time?"

Me: "Yes, Sir."

XO: "Oh great. Now she's gonna stink up the wardroom again. I hate that fluffy crap."

Me: "I replaced the banana truffle beans with vanilla-flavored ones, Sir."

Cap'n: "So, X, as I was saying . . . "

The crew is cleaning up and in the process finding old treasures. BM1 Hiatt has found the ship's stadimeter, a optical rangefinder used during World War II to estimate distances to ships. "In practice, a sailor would identify a distant ship, adjust the stadimeter for its mast-head height (a figure available in published accounts), bring the image of the mast-head into coincidence with the water line, and read the distance on the instrument's drum." (ref: Smithsonian)

In memory of George Keefer a staunch supporter of the Coast Guard, an avid photographer, and friend to me.

George Keefer and Sandy Planisek aboard the Mackinaw, November 2004.

About the Author

Sandy Planisek has been fortunate to live on the *Mackinaw* for extended periods during the past two years. During this time she met the crew, shared their interests, and learned about their specialties. It has been the opportunity of a lifetime and Sandy spent every minute collecting ideas, comments, and information for this book while making video tapes for the world-class museum *Mackinaw* is expected to become.

Sandy has written several other books the most recent being *Reliving Lighthouse Memories* also for the Great Lakes Lighthouse Keepers Association. Proceeds from the sale of these books go toward historic preservation.

Sandy with LTJG Lawrence. He is proof reading some of the pages of this book. Numerous crewmembers helped in writing this book by answering endless questions and reading the pages. They wanted the final days of Mackinaw's life recorded as much as Sandy did.